Incarcerated Stories

Incarcerated Stories

Indigenous Women Migrants and
Violence in the Settler-Capitalist State

Shannon Speed

The University of North Carolina Press CHAPEL HILL

This book was published with the assistance of the Anniversary Fund of the University of North Carolina Press.

Set in Merope Basic by Westchester Publishing Services
Manufactured in the United States of America

The University of North Carolina Press has been a member of the Green Press Initiative since 2003.

Library of Congress Cataloging-in-Publication Data
Names: Speed, Shannon, 1964–author.
Title: Incarcerated stories : indigenous women migrants and violence in
   the settler-capitalist state / Shannon Speed.
Other titles: Critical indigeneities.
Description: Chapel Hill : University of North Carolina Press, [2019] | Series:
   Critical indigeneities | Includes bibliographical references and index.
Identifiers: LCCN 2019008164| ISBN 9781469653112 (cloth : alk. paper) |
   ISBN 9781469653129 (pbk : alk. paper) | ISBN 9781469653136 (ebook)
Subjects: LCSH: Women—Effect of imprisonment on—United States. |
   Mexicans—Effect of imprisonment on—United States. | Central
   Americans—Effect of imprisonment on—United States. | Women—
   United States—Social conditions—21st century. | Mexicans—United
   States—Social Conditions—21st century. | Central Americans—
   United States—Social Conditions—21st century. | Women—United
   States—Economic Conditions—21st century. | Mexicans—United States—
   Economic Conditions—21st century. | Central Americans—United States—
   Economic Conditions—21st century.
Classification: LCC HV8738 .S63 2019 | DDC 362.83/9814092397073—dc23
   LC record available at https://lccn.loc.gov/2019008164

Cover illustration: Art by Micah Bazant. Originally commissioned by CultureStrike for the *Visions from the Inside* (2015) exhibition. Courtesy of the artist.

For my mother, Iris Speed

For all the brave women who confront
the structures of power daily in pursuit
of a life free of violence

Contents

Figures

Incarcerated Stories

CHAPTER ONE

Power and Vulnerability through Indigenous Women's Stories

Ysinia,[1] a Maya Mam woman from near Quetzaltenango, Guatemala, left home, fleeing a husband who beat her repeatedly and threatened to kill her. When his last beating nearly succeeded in realizing that threat, she made the difficult decision to leave, devastated to part with her family but in fear for her life. The trip north was not easy. She was detained by Mexican immigration agents who mocked her and questioned her about why an "Indita" would venture to leave her community—didn't she know it was dangerous? Farther north, in Reynosa, she was abducted by armed men and held in a house for ransom. There she witnessed another woman, who spoke a different Mayan language and very little Spanish, being brutally beaten by their captors for failing to get the required money. After Ysinia's ransom was paid, she was released and made her way to the border. However, after a very harrowing but ultimately successful crossing into the United States, the two men who she and others had paid to bring them across separated her from the group and tried to rape her. She fought back and her screams got the attention of others who came to her aid. Unfortunately, the ruckus created by the incident drew the attention of the border patrol and Ysinia was apprehended. When I met her, she was being held at the T. Don Hutto immigration detention facility in Taylor, Texas. Inside Hutto, she spoke of the unbearable tedium of the days that led her again and again to thoughts of all that has happened to her, the bitter sorrow of being separated from her children, and her struggle to fight off paralyzing fear and depression as she awaited her fate as an asylum seeker in the United States.

Indigenous women in the Americas are subject to extraordinary and systematically unseen levels of violence. This is true from the northern reaches of Canada and Alaska to the tip of Tierra del Fuego. Indigenous women migrants are emblematic of this social reality; their liminality as they move through social space renders them both vulnerable and invisible in a multiplicity of ways. The myriad forms of violence they suffer are neither random nor products of chance. Rather, they reflect the structural brutality of inequalities of gender, race, class, and nationality, linked to neoliberal logics in which market forces define social relations. Indigenous women

1

migrants' stories thus have much to tell us not only about violence but also about how state power is working in the current moment.

In this book, I depart from the oral histories of Indigenous women migrants from Mexico and Central America to provide an analysis of settler state power. Their stories are invariably compelling, reflecting both tremendous violence that shocks the conscience and human strength that boggles the mind. These women have suffered human rights violations at every step of their journey. Many experience domestic violence serious enough to compel them to leave home, community, and family, and to undertake a dangerous journey with an unknown outcome. Others undertake that precarious journey in an attempt to flee gang violence or cartel threats. Authorities in their home countries are unwilling or unable to protect them from this violence or to hold accountable those who perpetrate it. Their journey inevitably takes them through Mexico, where they may experience violence at the hands of human traffickers, petty criminals, gangs, and cartels, as well as the military, police, and immigration authorities. Once they enter the United States as immigrants, they face potential incarceration under draconian immigration laws and policies ostensibly designed to impede terrorism. Those who avoid detention but remain undocumented often face new vulnerability to violence at the hands of strangers or family members because of a fear of reporting. Indeed, violence so thoroughly marks the lives of Indigenous women migrants that it is hard for many to imagine a life in which they are not vulnerable to it.

That vulnerability is not a condition of the women themselves, but rather a structural condition. As I will show in the pages that follow, this condition was consciously created through the settler-colonial process, and, though functioning differently across space and time, consistently deploys racial and gender ideologies to manage the ongoing business of settler occupation. I use the terms *vulnerable* and *vulnerability* purposefully in this work. I am sympathetic to critiques of scholars like Sherene Razack who have signaled the potential consequences of using the term, which could include interpreting vulnerability as an existential condition and might then even imply blaming women for the violence they experience (this happened because they were vulnerable); underestimating women's agency (the women's lives are simply a product of structural forces); or taking the focus off the perpetrators (particularly the settler state) (see Razack 2016). However, I want to use the term here to do precisely the opposite, to reveal the multiple ways in which Indigenous women are rendered vulnerable to a range of perpetrators through structures of settler capitalist power, and act to resist by surviving.

Vulnerability as I discuss it here is not an inherent characteristic, but rather one imposed in multiple, intersecting ways as power is deployed in the world. In Spanish, this difference would be expressed by saying that, rather than being *vulnerables* (vulnerable), they are *vulneradas* (made vulnerable) by the structures of the settler-capitalist state. Butler, Gambetti, and Sabsay (2016) usefully discard the vulnerability–agency dichotomy and turn vulnerability on its head by making it a condition of resistance. While that will not be the main use of vulnerability in this book, I will return to it in the discussion of agency and resistance in the final chapter. My primary purpose is to reveal, through an examination of the ways Indigenous women migrants are *vulneradas*, the current contours of settler-capitalist state power.

Indigenous women have long experienced violence, but it has increased dramatically for them (as it has for many) in the current moment. This reality contrasts sharply with what was promised to many of Latin America's Indigenous people in the 1990s. As some nations in the region embraced globalization and neoliberal market reforms, many people expected a corresponding wave of democratization and expansion of rights.[2] As states undertook an often massive reorientation of their economies (Mexico is particularly notable), they ended land reforms, eliminated state subsidies for farming and industry, privatized capital and natural resources, limited tariffs on foreign goods, and slashed government social welfare programs. At the same time, they moved toward popularly elected governments and seemed to embrace expanded notions of human rights and the rule of law. A number of states, including Mexico and Guatemala, even reformed their constitutions to recognize Indigenous peoples and extend to them some level of collective Indigenous rights. Often posited as the inevitable spread of neoliberal democracy on a U.S. model (at times with an evolutionist flavor of development toward the highest state of being, one naturally epitomized by the United States), these processes seemed to offer at least some increase in political stability, rights, and accountability that are frequently discussed under the umbrella of recognition and rights regimes.

During this period of "democratic opening" in Latin America, theorists debated the benefits and limitations of these changes for Indigenous people. Some hailed the recognition of Indigenous peoples' rights as a significant victory "shaping the quality of democracy in Latin America" and signifying "a major power shift" and "a more generalized opening of the political system to excluded and vulnerable sectors of society" (Van Cott 2007:127; see also Van Cott 2000). Others signaled a need to "qualify somewhat premature and narrow discussion of democratic consolidation" (Yasher 1999:77). Analysts also sounded alarms about the ways in which multicultural rights regimes might work against Indigenous peoples, reinforcing state power and creating structures that, by focusing on collective identity rather than collective well-being, obscured the economic inequalities that were certain only to grow under neoliberalism.

Charles Hale (2005, 2006) particularly questioned the multiculturalism that underpinned the politics of recognition and tied it to neoliberalism, coining the term *neoliberal multiculturalism* as he warned of the dangers of an overinvestment in limited cultural rights at the expense of socioeconomic inequality. Hale (2002) also suggested that the limited rights afforded by neoliberal multiculturalism served to keep people focused on the possibility of qualifying for state-sponsored rights, rather than engaging in struggles for potentially more just systems of governance. Other theorists, myself among them, focused on the dangers for Indigenous people of relying on the state's legal regimes for their liberation and highlighted the multiple forms of state subject making at work in these arenas (García 2005; Hernandez, Paz, and Sierra 2004; Park and Richards 2007; Postero 2006; Sieder 2002; Speed 2005; Speed and Sierra 2005).[3] While all recognized the significance of the constitutional and political changes for Indigenous people, analysts busily debated how extensive and effective those were likely to be in contributing to greater equality or power for Indigenous peoples.

However, in a span of little more than a decade, we have seen a significant shift in the form of the state itself and its forms of governance. Since the 1990s, free market economies in Mexico and Central America quickly expanded and grew out of the control of legal regimes. Meanwhile, the nascent democratic tendencies and fledgling rights regimes, however limited, were quickly sucked into the vortex of the mass-scale illegal economies. Drug, gun, and human trafficking expanded as cartels grew in Mexico, feeding on widespread corruption of the government and military and the deregulated flows of capital. Cartels also found a reserve army in those newly impoverished under neoliberal reforms (Campbell 2009; Valdez Cárdenas 2011). In Guatemala, for example, "predatory economic and military elites" built an exclusionary state. A culture of violence left by war, combined with the increasing presence of organized crime cartels, led to weak reform and a surge in criminal and social violence (Briscoe and Rodríguez Pellecer 2010; Gavigan 2011:99). In the era of drug wars and the post-9/11 global "war on terror," the structural forces of neoliberalism combined with the emergence of the national security state. Increasingly, authoritarian and militarized governance became the new norm throughout Latin America. Human rights and Indigenous rights faded into obscurity in the face of obscene levels of bloodshed caused by social actors who carried out violence with impunity.

In that context, the women whose stories give form to this book left their homes and set out across Honduras, Guatemala, Mexico, and the United States in search of a life free of violence. By moving with these women migrants through space, I will explore how that violence remained. Ideologies of gender, race, class, and nationality function together with neoliberal market logics, and as a result, these women continue to confront violence at home, on their journey, and in the United States. Examining policing, detention, and human trafficking, I will draw conclusions about the condition of the nation-state, as well as those subject to its violence. I characterize this structural violence as *neoliberal multicriminalism*, and in the following pages I will reveal how it is related to the settler structures of Indigenous dispossession and elimination. I will argue that settler structures and neoliberal dynamics produce the vulnerability of Indigenous women migrants, rendering them subject to multiple violences.

Incarcerated Stories: Crossing Methodological, Geographical, and Theoretical Borders

The women in this book are from Mexico, Guatemala, and Honduras. These are countries with much in common; they also have many differences. In one sense, the reason for the focus on these countries is simple: they are the home countries of the women I met in immigration detention centers in the course of this project. The vast majority of immigrants crossing the southern border of the United States are from Mexico or Central America: in fiscal year 2017 they represented 95.5 percent of those apprehended by the U.S. Border Patrol.[4] They also represent the majority of people populating its immigration prisons.[5] Given my particular interest in the experiences of Indigenous women, I was put in contact less often with Salvadoran migrants, who have a smaller Indigenous migration pool, and thus I focus on the three nations just mentioned. The value of analyzing these countries together lies in the similarity of their experience historically and today. All three suffered European colonization, characterized by Indigenous dispossession and labor exploitation over several centuries. All experienced processes of neoliberalization in the 1990s, with related changes in governance patterns. And finally, all three countries have experienced surges in extreme violence in the last decade and a half, tied to illegal markets and organized crime, placing them at the top of the world rankings for murders and feminicide.

But to understand the impact of neoliberal multicriminalism, we must place the United States into the same analytical frame. The oft-reified divide between the United States and "Latin America" is more often than not a product of U.S. exceptionalism, and it is highly ideological. Extending well beyond an understanding that there are different (all settler-imposed) national languages and distinct legal systems, the ideological enters when the default assumption is that the United States is a well-functioning democracy in which law, order, and tolerance reign, while Latin American is characterized by corruption, illegality, and poorly functioning or weak democracy. I will argue that the United States is every bit as "multicriminal," in the sense of generating a context for, and lack of accountability for, violations of national and international laws and rights, as Mexico, Guatemala, or Honduras.

I have chosen to base this work on oral histories largely because of the nature of the project itself. While oral histories are not an unusual method for an anthropologist, earlier work produced from this research has engendered some critiques that ethnographic fieldwork in a particular "community" is not the major source of data and that traditional ethnographic description is not the primary narrative form.[6] However, given the nature of the "community"—Indigenous women migrants for whom the closest site as a center of gravity in this study is an immigration detention center—and, more importantly, the nature of the material (accounts of violence), oral histories are an ideal method, allowing the women to tell their stories and convey information from their own perspective.

Indeed, it was the stories themselves that gave rise to the project. In 2010 I began working with the Hutto Visitation Program, an organization that coordinates visits of volunteers to immigrant women detained in the T. Don Hutto immigration detention facility. The purpose of the nascent project was to provide human rights accompaniment to women in the infamous facility, which had recently been the target of a lawsuit against the Department of Homeland Security for detaining families in prisonlike conditions, as well as recently having had guards arrested and prosecuted for sexual abuse of women detainees. At that time, I was director of the Community Engagement Center at the University of Texas at Austin, which worked to generate collaborative research on critical social justice issues. Within the center, the Social Justice Institute run by scholar-activist Eric Tang channeled support to nascent community-generated projects. The Hutto Visitation Program was one of these projects. It was formed by community activists, particularly the organizations Grassroots Leadership and Texans United for Families, both of which had long been active in advocating for the rights of immigrants in detention and opposing detention itself, in response to the need to monitor human rights conditions inside the T. Don Hutto facility and to provide accompaniment to the women housed there. Volunteers from all walks of life visit with women in the facility, providing friendship, solidarity, and a link to the outside world.

I was particularly compelled to engage in this work by reports that there were a significant number of Indigenous women from Latin America in the facility, many of them with limited levels of Spanish ability. The reports conjured a terrible picture in my mind of the Tzeltal, Tzotzil, and Chol women I had worked with over the years in Chiapas, incarcerated in such an alien and frightening place. As I began to visit, one thing that quickly became clear to me was that the women want—indeed need—to tell their stories. It is cathartic for them to relate their experiences, gratifying to know that other people care about them, and comforting to hear, through the stories of others, that they are not alone in what they have experienced. As I spoke with women in Hutto, as well as later at the Karnes County Residential Center when family detention was reestablished, I came to understand that in many senses, their power to control their own lives had been taken from them repeatedly through acts of violence, and that telling their stories allowed them to recover control of that past.

Yet the task of telling such stories is profoundly challenging. Most of these stories were collected under physically and emotionally trying circumstances in the cold, sterile space of detention center visitation rooms. Visitors are not allowed to bring anything at all into the detention center, which meant I was without as much as a pencil or scrap of paper, let alone recording equipment. When I began trying to make a record of the stories, I would exit the detention center and sit in my car in the parking lot, writing down everything I could remember. The next time I visited, I would ask questions, fill in gaps. Over time, the stories surfaced on the paper, smuggled, quite literally, out of the detention center inside my brain. Like the women who lived them, the stories were truly incarcerated, and gaining their release felt like a very real form of resistance. Indeed, even the stories told here of women whom I met outside the detention centers (there are two) constitute incarcerated stories, in the sense that they are not normally heard, are locked away and silenced, and reflect the women's entrapment in the structural cages of the settler capitalist state. The structures and institutions that serve to render all migrants' experiences invisible exert significant power to cage both women and their stories. For reasons that I will explore, Indigenous women migrants are particularly vulnerable to this caging.[7] Gathering their stories and telling them feels like a way to contest that power.

I also tell these stories from within what is arguably the most colonized and colonizing of disciplines. Anthropology was birthed from the colonial project; the undertaking of anthropological representation itself constituted the quintessential violence of transforming sovereign human beings into the colonizable Others of "civilization." At least since Vine Deloria Jr. declared that "Indians have been cursed above all other people in history. Indians have anthropologists" (1969:78) and characterized anthropologists as "forerunners of destruction . . . intolerably certain that they represent ultimate truth" (1969:100), the coloniality of anthropology[8] for Native peoples has been blisteringly clear. In the intervening years—not really because of Indian critiques but rather because of theoretical interventions emanating from European intellectuals regarding the nature of "truth" in modernity and postmodernity—anthropologists have engaged in considerable hand-wringing regarding our representations. Anthropologists have focused overly, in my view, on the subjective nature of observation and analysis (which should be a given), and the proffered solutions have been to "situate ourselves" (acknowledging our subjective location) or to seek recourse in the textual (there is no Truth, so all writing is fiction), rather than a much-needed critical engagement with the politics of knowledge production (the understanding that all knowledge produced has political effects on its subjects). In other words, anthropologists largely continue to sidestep the simple question Deloria posed regarding anthropological research nearly fifty years ago: "The question for Indian people, and the ultimate question for Americans, is: What effect will it have over the lives of people?" (1969:99).[9]

In the past I have argued for the value of a *critically engaged activist research* that combines critical analysis and overt commitment to an engagement with our research participants that is directed toward some form of shared social justice goals in a way that is doubly accountable, not only to further our theoretical understanding of social dynamics but also to advance concrete objectives in the lives of those we work with (Speed 2006, 2008b). I believe this is true for all anthropologists, but perhaps even more so for Indigenous anthropologists working with Indigenous people, as we face a pressing imperative to decolonize our research or, at a minimum, not to recolonize ourselves in the research process (L. T. Smith 1996; A. W. Wilson and Yellow Bird 2005; 2012). This means not just taking Indigenous peoples' experience seriously but also taking *their understanding* of it seriously, while putting that in dialogue with the researchers' own critical analysis and directing them consciously toward some type of shared end that is of use in peoples' lives.[10]

Oral history itself is a contested field. There are many debates in the field of oral history and *testimonio* regarding the merits of verbatim transcription, editing, contextualizing, and, above all, analyzing. Institutional review boards in the United States, for example, take oral history to be such a restricted field (literally recording people's memories and preserving them) that it does not constitute "research" and thus is not subject to human subjects review.[11] This is problematic because, as Blackwell argues, "testimonio and oral history are often received . . . as the supposedly pure Other or subaltern through a supposedly unmediated narrative instead of considering the politics of production involved and the political strategies of the narrators" (2011:42). But acknowledging the politics of that knowledge production for both the research subjects and the researcher causes many oral historians discomfort. There has been a fair amount of deliberation about how oral history and testimony works as "data" and particularly whether peoples' oral recountings can or should be taken as truth, given the vicissitudes of memory.[12]

In general, Indigenous feminists have tended to be less concerned with such questions, for several reasons: we tend to be more comfortable—without falling into facile stereotypes—with storytelling as a mode of knowledge transferal (Archibald 2008; A. C. Wilson 1996); we tend not to be invested in hierarchically positioned Western positivist notions of truth (L. T. Smith 1999; Yellow Bird 2005); and, relatedly, we tend to hold Indigenous women's experience and its telling as both a political act and a valid form of theorization (Archuleta 2006). In the late 1980s and early 1990s, Native women writers began to emphasize the significance of Native women's stories for shedding light on larger sociopolitical and historical dynamics. In *Writing as Witness*, Mohawk author Beth Brant (1995) argues that all Native writings, but particularly Native women's stories, are by their very nature political and contestatory to the colonial structures and legacies that silence Indigenous voices and invisibilize our collective experience. Spokane writer Gloria Bird made similarly powerful arguments in "Breaking the Silence: Writing as 'Witness'" (1997). More recently, Mishuana Goeman, in *Mark My Words*, argues for the significance of taking Native women's literature seriously: "By examining Native women writers through an intersectional approach, I am choosing a feminist method of analysis that presents us with a multiple grounded 'telling' of violence and its impact on the structural, political, and representational lives of Native peoples and their communities" (2013:14). Literature is different from oral history, of course, but my argument is that Indigenous women's stories, in literature or other forms, provide a grounded telling of violence that is otherwise silenced. Dian Million, in her influential essay "Felt Theory," extends this argument and demonstrates how First Nations women in Canada, "by insisting on the inclusion of our lived experience, rich with emotional knowledges," reframed what could be known and talked about in relation to the collective experience of boarding schools in Canada (2009:54). In a somewhat similar vein, Maylei Blackwell also emphasizes the differential knowledge Native women bring through their lived experience, especially of experiences long occluded in official history: "Through [subaltern women's oral histories] a different way of knowing or new epistemologies are introduced into the (warped) historical record" (2011:39). In other words, telling Indigenous women's stories is important because through them, the largely invisibilized social processes of colonization are rendered visible, and from a distinct ideological perspective. Thus, my interest is not to provide a history that is testable and verifiably "true" in some abstract sense. Nor am I particularly interested in deconstructing women's testimony in order to show how one or another thing has led them to remember or recount in "incorrect" ways.[13] The women's memory of their experience is itself the *embodied experience* of what has happened to them, and in that sense it is the "real" story I am interested in, and which I believe presents a source of knowledge not bound by hegemonic ideological frames.

While I do not analyze Indigenous women migrants' stories in the deconstructive sense, I am interested in being attentive to and writing about what they tell us regarding how race, class, and gender are working in the current neoliberal context. These ideologies shape what experiences the women have, marking them, I argue, for violence at every step. More to the point, they also shape how women experience events in their lives, and how they remember those experiences. It is thus also crucial that we ask how gender, race, and class, as structural and ideological relations, shape the construction of historical memory, not to make claims *about* their stories (as true or false, etc.) but rather to make claims *from* their stories.[14] Lynn Stephen argues that "oral testimony as an embodied speech act permits people to represent personal histories within fused/inseparable identity categories of gender, race, ethnicity, class, sexuality and more" (2015:9). The women's stories often in this way bypass the categorizations so prevalent in Western academic theorizing—of "race" as analytically separable from "gender" and so on—which inevitably invisibilize Indigenous women, and instead, departing from their complex self-representations, offer new ways to think about the fields in which they are multiply constituted as social actors.[15]

However, the women's stories presented here are not being presented by them in the sense that Bird, Brant, or Million discussed. They are all my representations, mediated by my role as author; in many cases, they are my memories of their memories. In *Violence and the Limits of Representation*, Matthews and Goodman (2013) make a compelling argument for the importance of thinking critically about the ways in which violence is framed, mediated, and regulated through representations. As a Native feminist, I was highly cognizant of the increased dangers when representing Indigenous women and gender violence because of the dual potential for anthropological representations to "delve into two central western fantasies—the eroticization of domination and the eroticization of 'the (dominated) Other'" (Harvey and Gow 2013:2). Yet the ways the women were marked for violence in multiple forms and in many contexts was precisely what I, as a Native feminist analyst, found compelling about their stories.

Perhaps even more fundamental than the issue of how to represent the women was the issue of whether or why I should represent them. As a survivor of violence myself, the women's stories literally reverberated in my body, in much the same way as every feminicidal image of women's and girls' violated bodies, tossed out on roadsides and empty fields like so much waste, physically hits me. Those who have experienced trauma are familiar with its psychophysical manifestation, its affective impact. I felt as if I had suffered the actual trauma anew in some small way each time. Driving home from the detention center or other meeting place, feeling vaguely nauseous and oddly disconnected from my own embodied reality, I asked myself, why I was subjecting myself to this. Why hear these stories, why tell them? This was not a rhetorical question, and while deeply personal, it was also an intellectual, analytical question. Should we talk about and hear about terrible experiences of violence? In a *New York Times* op-ed, Saïd Sayrafiezadeh debated the value of "writing about trauma."[16] I have wrestled considerably with the dual questions of whether and how to write about women's stories of violence and do so in ways that convey the full weight of their experience—with all of the pain, fear, and anguish that attends such violent experiences—yet not engage in what might be termed "pornographics of violence," rendering their stories little more than titillating entertainment for those privileged enough never to experience it. Sayrafiezadeh's opinion piece reached its teaching moment when the author came to a key realization about the reasons for telling stories of trauma: that they represent our collective and overarching *vulnerability*—that is, their telling can lead us to a larger understanding, which is precisely my goal. In telling these difficult stories, I seek to understand broader dynamics that generate the violence against Indigenous women migrants, and specifically how neoliberal settler power works by rendering certain subjects multiply vulnerable.[17] It is a story rarely told, and one that needs to be heard.

Thinking Hemispherically: Bridging the Work on Native North and South

I transgress several disciplinary boundaries in this book. The first border (and the one that has most vexed me over the years) is that of the literatures on Native North and South. As a Chickasaw, I am a citizen of a tribal nation based in the United States, but I have worked for much of my professional life with Indigenous people in Latin America, particularly Mexico. I have a strong tendency to think hemispherically and to see a great deal of shared experience among Indigenous people generally, and Indigenous women specifically, despite the oft-repeated truisms of distinct colonial histories, relations with the state, and so on. The fact that the literature is sharply divided into Native American Studies and Indigenous Latin American Studies is unproductive at best. Indigenous women migrants, as border crossers whose experience takes place in both North and South, provide an interesting opportunity to examine dynamics across a space that is, in many senses, arbitrarily divided in both practical and intellectual terms.

Notably, because "qualifying" as Indigenous in the United States is premised largely on belonging to a group that the federal government recognizes as a tribe. Despite the multiple and serious problems this entails Indigenous people from Latin America cannot and will not ever fully "qualify" as Indigenous once they have entered the United States. From the time they cross the border, they are engaged by the state only as "Mexican nationals" or "Guatemalan nationals," which effectively erases their Indigenous identity.[18] From this perspective, it would make far more sense to approach Indigenous women migrants from the literature on immigration and immigrants, rather than that of Indigenous studies. However, Indigenous identity is not something that vanishes when moving through space. Indigenous peoples of this continent have long experienced mobility (forced or otherwise), including before European invasion, and they have remained Indigenous people. The erasure of Indigenous migrants' identity as Indigenous people is one in a long series of technologies used by settler states to eliminate Indigenous people, and as scholars we should not participate in reifying settler-imposed national borders in ways that facilitate such erasures.

Anthropologists, to their credit, have generally understood that Indigenous people remain Indigenous in migration, and much of that literature is dedicated to exploring what continues to define them as Indigenous once they are in the United States. Some have analyzed the way that Indigenous migrants organize around identities such as Mixtecos, Zapotecos, or Maya, developing binational ties to home communities, moving back and forth between communities, or reformulating cultural practices in their new communities in the United States (Fox and Rivera-Salgado 2004b; Foxen 2008; Kearny 1995; MacKenzie 2016; Rosas 2012; Stephen 2007; Velasquez Orozco 2005). Others have explored how migration affects cultural practices and political processes in migrants' home communities in Mexico or Central America (Aquino Moreschi 2009; Burrell 2005). These works have provided important insights on the experience of migration for Indigenous people from Latin America, yet they are principally concerned with immigrants who have entered a stable (and usually sizable) community and do not address the experience of Indigenous people who are still in motion or are otherwise unsettled.

A few studies have productively focused on the process of migration itself (De Leon 2015; Holmes 2013; Vogt 2013, 2015). While this is a promising trend that has generated outstanding scholarship highlighting the structural violence in play in the migration process, this work has focused largely on non-Indigenous male experience (Vogt 2016 is an exception). De Leon notes (albeit not until chapter 10) the "paucity of research" of women border crossers, which he attributes to both "male bias" and the fact that "women typically make up less than 15% of the migrant pool" (2015:246). Nevertheless, he shows that women disproportionately suffer death at the border—in fact, they are 2.67 times more likely to die of exposure in the desert than men. Vogt's (2016) work on the Central American migrant trail through Mexico also emphasizes that women migrants experience a higher level of vulnerability to sexual violence than men. Thus, a sustained focus on women's experience is important for shedding light on the intersections of race and gender in the structures that render migrants vulnerable to violence and death. Another missing element in all of the aforementioned authors' analyses is that issues of Indigenous dispossession, settler structures, and even capitalism (in Holmes and De Leon) are absent or undertheorized, leading to an overemphasis on U.S. policy without an analysis of the structures that policy is defined within. My work addresses these structural features that shape the lives of Indigenous women migrants.

In later chapters, I draw on the work of crimmigration scholars who focus on how structural elements like the law work to render particular subjects vulnerable to harm, and particularly how laws and policies are designed to control and to limit certain populations based on race and related criteria (García Hernández 2017; Guia, Woude, and Leun 2013; Stumpf 2006). However, because of the nature of this field (legal studies), these works often leave the human subjects of these dynamics in the abstract. From sociology, Menjívar and Abrego (2012) bring the people back as they examine how law — particularly immigration law — constitutes "legal violence" that generates vulnerability and direct harm to particular subjects. These studies help to frame my understanding of structural vulnerability through law.

I also draw on the work of scholars in critical Latinx Indigeneities, who have analyzed the growing Indigenous Latin American diaspora, with a focus on "the colonial legacies at play across the transregions created by Indigenous migration" (Blackwell, Boj López, and Urrieta 2017:127). These scholars contest the idea that when Indigenous people migrate, they lose their Indigeneity, and acknowledge the new and old structural dynamics designed to manage and erase Indigeneity with which migrant populations are forced to contend. However, rather than positing Latinx studies as the intellectual space for studying Indigeneity (though of course it can and should be), I suggest that Indigenous studies can provide the intellectual space to think about migration because of the insight that Indigenous migration provides into larger settler structures.

While this book's protagonists are migrants, I do not understand its contribution to be primarily about immigration. Instead, it is the structural situatedness of Indigenous women migrants, and their liminality as they move through space, that reveals the settler-capitalist structures in which their lives and their migrations are enmeshed. Nevertheless, my work here draws on much of the aforementioned literature, while exploring Indigenous women's experience in the migration process through an Indigenous studies lens.

However, my aspiration is not limited to encouraging greater engagement within Indigenous studies with Indigenous migration from the South. I would like to see greater engagement with the South itself. The separation of Indigenous studies literatures into North and South is premised on the understanding that the two regions of the hemisphere are the result of distinct colonial experiences: Anglophone and Hispanic (thus Mexico is always included in the "South" despite its geographical location in North America). Clearly, there are significant differences. The United States and Latin American countries are distinct in national language, histories of state-Indigenous relations, and legal traditions. In the United States, tribes were recognized by European colonizers as sovereign nations, and as the U.S. government forcibly relocated tribes and dissolved their governments, a "trust" relationship was established that has defined state-Indigenous relations. In Latin America, European colonizers did not recognize Indigenous peoples' sovereignty and they were instead made subjects of the Spanish Crown; then, three hundred years later, they became colonized citizen populations of newly independent settler states. It has been a generally accepted truism that the goals of colonization in the United States and Latin America were fundamentally distinct: in the North, focused on land dispossession and the correlated elimination of the Native, and in the South, focused on resource extraction and the correlated marshaling and control of Indigenous labor (see, for example, Wolfe 1998:1).

Yet while in the broadest sense this truism is not entirely incorrect, like most truisms it is limited. Painting these regions with such a broad brush tends to gloss over significant similarities in how colonialism unfolded: Indigenous labor was also marshaled in the United States, for example, and the resource and labor extraction that characterized much of the Latin American experience were premised fundamentally on dispossession. Considering "North" and "South" in such broad terms also overlooks notable differentiation in experiences within Latin America, where both colonial powers and the neocolonial state differed substantially in logics and practice (again, Mexico and Guatemala are a good example of this, particularly in the modern-state period, with vastly different racialization schemes underpinning their colonial control).

Due to the fact that analysts have tended to emphasize the differences in colonial processes in the United States and Latin America, they tend to overlook many similarities of experience. Further, they forgo important opportunities to engage theoretically, leaving us with often insular debates that might benefit from cross-dialogue. There is what I view as a dual theoretical gap in regard to state theorizations: theorizations of the settler state have not grappled fully enough with neoliberal capitalism, and theories of the neoliberal state fail to recognize the significance of settler logics that structure the conditions of state formation, including in its current neoliberal iteration. In this book, I strive to put these literatures and experiences in dialogue in generative ways, taking the United States, Mexico, Guatemala, and Honduras into the framing. Four countries is a lot to take on in one work, at least for an anthropologist, but it is my hope that the hemispheric dialogue will be fruitful enough to outweigh any loss of detail pertaining to each place.

Theoretical Interventions: Gender Violence, Neoliberalism, and the Colonial State

There are three overarching theoretical fields that will be engaged in this book: gender violence, settler-colonial states, and neoliberal regimes. While these may appear to be disparate subjects, my argument is that they are so heavily interrelated as to be analytically inseparable. That said, they do exist as separate sets of analytical debates, a situation I believe undermines our ability to fully understand their workings. In my understanding, they are all part of an overarching structure of power that renders Indigenous women vulnerable in particular ways in specific contexts.

Studies abound that demonstrate gender violence is at crisis levels in Native communities worldwide (for example, Amnesty International 2008 [United States]; Bachman et al. 2008 [United States]; Keel 2004 [Australia]; Canada National Clearinghouse 2008). According to the Indian Law Resource Center, in the United States, Indian women are two and a half times more likely to be assaulted and more than twice as likely to be stalked as other women. One in three Native women will be raped in her lifetime, and six in ten will be physically assaulted. On some reservations, the murder rate for Native women is ten times the national average. According to the research of the National Institute of Justice, four of five Native women experience violence in her lifetime, and 97 percent of these crimes are committed by non-Indians (Rosay 2018). Until very recently, tribal governments lacked any criminal jurisdiction over non-Indians under U.S. law, in spite of the fact that, according to the U.S. Census Bureau, 77 percent of the population residing on Indian lands and reservations is non-Indian (Rosay 2018; Indian Law Resource Center). Deer (2005) offers a similar set of statistics drawn from the National Crime Victimization Survey and the National Violence against Women Survey.

For Indigenous women in Mexico and Central America, statistics are scarce and underreporting is extensive. Nevertheless, the statistics we do have are worth noting. In Mexico, the government reported that in 2016, nearly two-thirds of Indigenous women reported experiencing violence

(66.1 percent) (Comisión Nacional para el Desarrollo de los Pueblos Indígenas 2016). In all categories of violence (physical, emotional, economic, and sexual), Indigenous women reported higher rates than non-Indigenous women, with emotional abuse being the highest: 49 percent of Indigenous and 45.5 percent of non-Indigenous women report experiencing it, and sexual violence shows the greatest differential, with 41.3 percent of Indigenous women compared to 29.6 percent of non-Indigenous women (Comisión Nacional para el Desarrollo de los Pueblos Indígenas 2016). In Honduras in 2017, a woman was violently murdered every fifteen hours (Observatorio Nacional de la Violencia de la Universidad Nacional Autónoma de Honduras 2018). In Guatemala, while all reports agree that the violence against women is severe, official numbers vary and are suspiciously low for a country in which a woman is murdered every seventeen hours. The state's own statistics bureau reported that in 86 percent of reported cases, they had no idea what the woman's identity or native language was (Instituto Nacional de Estadistica 2017). Clearly, violence against Indigenous women is a matter of pressing concern.

Though interpersonal violence, criminal violence, and state violence are often understood as distinct dynamics, I will argue that they are in fact interrelated, and, to some extent, mutually constituted. Domestic violence, which includes interfamilial and partner violence, by its very definition as "domestic," tends to be differentiated from other "public" forms of violence, and all too often it results in individual or (particularly Indigenous) community pathologizing that is focused on how to fix (or penalize) men while letting the state off the hook. Similarly, analyses of wartime sexual violence tend to focus on state actors and fail to draw connections between these and other forms of violence. But the women's stories in this study show, repeatedly, how these forms of violence are inseparable, each bound to the other and mutually formative in the larger context in which they affect the women's lives. Understanding that context is what necessitates an examination of the larger structures of power that render them vulnerable.

While this book is not posited as an intervention in the ample and important literature on structural violence (Anglin 1998; Benson 2008; Bourgois and Scheper Hughes 2004; Farmer 2004; Galtung 1969; Gupta 2012; Price 2012), it does have much in common with that field.

Coming largely from the field of medical anthropology, these studies have been concerned with forms of social suffering and everyday violence that are caused by structures of inequality. My work aligns with this objective, as I am concerned with how structural violence is rendered on the bodies and minds of Indigenous women migrants. However, I am interested not just in the existence of structural violence, which often appears as amorphous and nonspecific "power," but rather in a particular kind of structural violence: that of settler capitalism. Crenshaw's notion of structural intersectionality is useful here, as it allows me to explore the multiple layers of violence Indigenous women experience from their particular locations at the intersection of race, gender, and class (Crenshaw 1991; see also Price 2012; Riddle 2017). Approaching the analysis through Indigenous women's lived experience of these hierarchies of oppression allows them to reveal the specific structures of settler capitalism.

Theories of settler colonialism have been little applied in Latin America, focused as they are on Anglophone colonization.[19] However, the central precepts of settler colonialism set out by Wolfe —"The colonizers come to stay, invasion is a structure, not an event" (1999:2) — are spot on with regard to Latin America. Unlike metropole or administrative colonialism, in which the colonizer controls from afar with local agents on the ground, then retreats with independence, leaving the territory changed but essentially in the hands of the original peoples (e.g., India, parts of Africa), in Latin America the colonizers came to stay. And dispossess they did. It might then be worth applying a settler colonial analytic to this region.

In applying such a lens to Mexico and Central America, my goal is to trace the structures, technologies, and practices that characterize the enduring settler-colonial logics in Mexico and Central America (see Castellanos 2017). I do so to shed light on the workings of power in these spaces, not simply to mold settler-colonial theory to fit a particular space, as Shona Jackson (2012) has cautioned against. What I want to show is how spaces north and south of the border are in essence "settler," and what it means for Indigenous women migrants to move between distinct settler spaces. In *The Transit of Empire*, Jodi Byrd used the term *arrivant* to refer to "those people forced into the Americas through the violence of European and Anglo-American colonialism and imperialism" (2011:xix). Nowhere is this process clearer than in the current juncture, in which Indigenous Central American and Mexican refugees, fleeing the economic and political violence of what I call neoliberal multicriminalism — shaped as it is by neoliberalism and U.S. imperialism — transit from one settler structure to another. But Byrd was talking largely about non-Indigenous arrivants. I want to consider what happens when the arrivants are Indigenous people from within distinct settler-imposed nation-state boundaries. To understand these dynamics, I will need to examine settler-colonial histories (always already constituted in relation to Indigenous histories) in national settings in which they have rarely been examined. But in doing so, I endeavor to shed light on the interrelated—in fact, inseparable—workings of capitalism and U.S. imperialism, and the ways that ideologies of race and gender work to both facilitate and normalize the forms of oppression within these structures of power.

One of the reasons Latin America has been thought to be characterized by colonialism of the nonsettler variety is the perception that the goals of colonization there were distinct. While colonial processes in the North focused on land dispossession and the correlated elimination of the native, in the South, the colony was focused on resource extraction and the correlated marshaling and control of Indigenous labor. Yet much of Latin America has in fact been characterized by both: Indigenous land dispossession was a fundamental aspect of colonialism, combined with various regimes of labor extraction. In places like Mexico and Central America, such labor regimes were in fact the mechanism that dispossessed Indigenous peoples of their lands, forcing them to labor in extractive undertakings on the very land that had been taken from them. The binary logic of the land-labor divide is fundamentally flawed, and much of Latin America demonstrates that. The distinction between colonialism based on land and that based on labor was raised famously by Wolfe (1999) to signal a distinction that is more profound: that the underlying logics structuring societies based on different types of colonialism give rise to distinct social relations, forms of oppression, and affective understandings and subjectivities. In a general sense, in extractive regimes there is an inherent impetus to maintain and control the productive power of a labor force, and thus ongoing subordination operationalizes social relations. In settler regimes, the underlying impetus is "destroy to replace," and a logic of elimination rather than subordination is operative. The teleological argument that if colonialism involves labor extraction, it is not then, by definition, "settler" doesn't explain how labor extraction intersects with the "staying" settlers' dispossession of Indigenous people and the undeniable logic of elimination at work in much of the region, and increasingly so over time.

Of course, the initial period after European arrival in Mesoamerica entailed large-scale eliminations. An area as densely populated as Central Mexico, with twenty million inhabitants, could not be effectively occupied and transformed without them. If the "demographic disaster" of the sixteenth century (McCaa 2000:242)—that is, the death of possibly 90 percent of the Native population over a period of one hundred years—does not constitute elimination, it would be hard to say what does.[20] Yet, as Restall, Sousa, and Terraciano (2005) argue, enough people remained to significantly outnumber the Spaniards, and thus elaborate systems of management were necessitated.

Dispossession also began shortly after European arrival. In the Viceroyalty of New Spain, which included large swaths of the Caribbean, all of present-day Mexico, and most of present-day Central America (as well as much of the present-day United States),[21] a systematic policy of dispossession called *reducciones de indios* (Indian reductions) was put in place. The *reducciones* began as early as 1503 in the Caribbean, and in Mexico[22] shortly after Hernando Cortes's victory in the Valley of México in the 1520s (they were extended later to Baja California and California in the seventeenth and eighteenth centuries, respectively). In the *reducciones*, Indian populations were physically relocated from their ancestral lands into towns or villages created by the Spaniards for the purposes of evangelization and colonial control. As most writing on the colonial period in New Spain has highlighted, the concentration of the Native population—particularly in ways that purposefully ruptured kinship and tribal ties—facilitated control of their minds and bodies, increased access to their forced labor and forced tribute, and diminished their possibilities for resistance (Diaz Polanco 1997). Less emphasized has been the ways this dispossession facilitated ideological arguments and later laws about ostensibly unused lands—*tierras baldias*, which were deemed *tierras nulas*—uninhabited and wide open for the taking.

But elimination and dispossession are always incomplete projects. Veracini argues that "geographically, settler colonialism is premised on a displacement that is ultimately a non-displacement. Settlers transform geography" (2013b:1). In New Spain, Native villages were destroyed and new towns constructed on top of them that mimicked settlements in Spain. Mexico City itself, the capital of New Spain, was built atop the ruins of Tenochtitlan, once a beautiful and teeming metropolis and capital of the Mexica (Aztec) Empire. This was not just symbolic of replacement, but clearly *settler* replacement of the Native, as the geography itself was fundamentally transformed to reflect the (ostensible) permanence of settler occupation.

On this new landscape, Indigenous peoples were controlled through systems of slavery and enforced labor known as *encomienda* and *repartimiento*. Throughout the sixteenth century, settlers were granted groups of Natives, often whole polities, for the purposes of extracting tribute in goods and labor. In the seventeenth century, the *encomienda* was replaced with *repartimiento*, in which a Spanish settler or official would be given a number of Indigenous workers to "supervise" their labor in farms or mines. While they were required under *repartimiento* to pay the laborers, in practice this was a system of enforced labor. It contributed further to dispossession, as laborers were relocated to large haciendas or fled their communities to escape indentured servitude.

As in other parts of the Americas, much of the colonial period in New Spain was characterized by tensions between the metropole and the settlers— the Crown and the *Peninsulares*[23] and *Criollos*.[24] The Crown continually worked to rein in the authority of the *encomenderos*, and a series of laws were established to facilitate ongoing Spanish control from the metropole (Diaz Polanco 1991). This resulted in the Crown making Native people subjects (and thus rights holders), in no small part to check the power of the settlers. That these tensions existed is emblematic of the fundamentally "settler" character of colonization in Latin America. It was always the settler who most threatened Indigenous peoples in Latin America, not the colonial metropole. As Sierra and Seider (2010) describe, before independence, Spanish rule was characterized by a multiplicity of parallel Indigenous governance structures that were formalized in the *Leyes de Indios* (Indian Laws). These established a separate, subordinate legal jurisdiction for Indigenous subjects of the Spanish Crown within which Indigenous *usos y costumbres* (uses and customs) were operative. Castro and Picq (2017) analyze how Maya communities in Guatemala used these spaces to maintain their authority and also to litigate territorial sovereignty with the Crown.

Prior to independence, this type of indirect rule facilitated colonial domination of linguistically and culturally diverse Indigenous populations. However, after independence Indigenous people became citizens and were subject to the newly established unitary legal systems of the nascent republics. De jure recognition of semiautonomous legal spheres for the Indigenous population and statutory law in Mexico and Central America dictated that all inhabitants of the new republics be subject to the same legal regime. Writing of the Anglophone settler states, Lisa Ford argues that, "Before the War of 1812 in America . . . any attempt to define state sovereignty as a territorial measure effected through the exercise of jurisdiction foundered on the plurality of Indigenous legal status" (2010:129). She argues that "settler polities extended jurisdiction [over Indigenous peoples] in the 1820s and 1830s because they imagined for the first time that it was necessary to shore up the legitimacy of settlement" (2010:3). This same process was underway in Latin America in the same time period, as newly independent nation-states sought to establish their sovereignty and control over the populations within their territories, in part by extending legal jurisdiction over them. Thus, it is by means of independence that Indigenous peoples are legally "eliminated" as an existent population within the structures and logics of settler sovereignty.

Richard Gott is one of the few analysts who have argued in favor of understanding Latin America as a settler society. He states,

> The characteristics of white settler states of the European empires are generally familiar. The settlers sought to expropriate the land, and to evict or exterminate the existing population; they sought where possible to exploit the surviving Indigenous labor force to work on the land; they sought to secure for themselves a European standard of living; to justify or make sense of their global migration; they treated the Indigenous peoples with extreme prejudice, drafting laws to ensure that those who survived the wars of extermination remained largely without rights, as second or third class citizens. Latin America shares all of these characteristics and clearly falls into the category of "settler colonialism," even though the colonial powers are no longer present, having been forced out in the course of the nineteenth century. (2007:273)

Gott locates the birth of the settler Latin American state with independence, when outside settlers gained control of the Native population and its land. Importantly, he contests the prevailing notion in Latin America that colonialism ended with independence, which leads most theorists to view current conditions as neocolonial, "internal colonialism" (Gonzalez Casanova, Rivera Cusicanqui), or "coloniality" (Quijano, Mignolo), theories that seek to address the ongoing colonial nature of power relations but that view it as residual or a legacy of past colonialism, rather than an ongoing occupation. This point particularly matters for Indigenous people not only because it is inaccurate, but also because of the counterpart narrative that Kauanui has highlighted in relation to the United States, "the myth that Indigenous peoples ended when colonialism ended" (Kauanui 2016:1). While theorists of internal colonialism or coloniality of power certainly are not perpetrators of that myth, it can be said to have been the prevailing one in much of Latin America until at least the 1990s, when the quincentenary protests of 1992 and major revolts such as the Zapatista uprising in Chiapas took non-Indigenous people and their governments throughout the hemisphere by surprise. The problem with internal colonialism and coloniality of power analyses (and I do not mean to conflate the two; they are distinct positions and emerge from distinct positionalities that are significant and are discussed elsewhere in the book) is that by failing to address settler colonialism as such, they accept both the basic premise of independence and the premise of settlement: that the settler has settled and is now *from here*. Colonial relations are then internal, rather than an external imposition.

Also with independence, as Indigenous peoples were recast as individual citizens before law, racialization processes shifted. Another aspect of the distinction between the Anglophone and Hispanophone colonial processes in the Americas has been the idea that because of racial mixing, Latin America was not characterized by white settlement. The argument here is that unlike other places, in Latin America racial mixing led to a mixed-race population of Indigenous and Spaniard and that, therefore, colonizer and Native are genetically entwined and there is no racial separation of the two. This unfortunately conflates myth with reality. *Mestizaje* was a racial ideology consciously put forward by *criollo* elites seeking to consolidate the national identity of newly "independent" states characterized by the presence of large and diverse populations who did not identify as "Mexican" or "Central American"[25] and who had been dispossessed of their lands to make way for these states and their *criollo* rulers—the settlers. The logic of elimination was very much at work in this process, and in ways that were remarkably similar to those operating in the United States, from independence on (indeed, Latin American settlers were importing their ideas from the United States). They were, in many parts of the continent (especially in Mexico) extremely successful in propagating this myth. Natividad Gutierrez refers to this as the "façade of the ideologized fusion of two cultural traditions, the Spanish and the native, officially imposed on the heterogeneous Mexican community," which happened so successfully that "90 per cent of the country's population is now considered mestizo" (1995:161).

Saldaña Portillo (2016) traces the different racialization processes taking place in Mesoamerica and what would become the United States, highlighting the ways that different racial categories served distinct but coordinated colonial ends and, far from describing racial difference, in fact productively constituted it (see also Wolfe 2016:10). While analysts have tended to view the hegemony of the *mestizaje* ideology as something that distinguishes it from the U.S. experience, it is also true that racial mixing as an assimilationist strategy of elimination became a force in practice in most Latin American countries at the same time that it did in the United States (in the mid-nineteenth century), enjoyed its strongest period in the early part of the twentieth century, and was deployed in strikingly similar ways and directed to the same ends of elimination. The major difference—as Saldaña Portillo elucidates—was that Latin American states discursively retained Indigeneity as part of the identity mix (albeit in ways that rendered living Indians a part of the historic past), while in the United States indigeneity was discursively eliminated (by mixing with whites, Indians literally disappeared). This has played out differently in different countries, of course: Mexico is notably different from Guatemala, where settler culture lent itself to a more apartheid regime, leading eventually to genocide in the later twentieth century. In other countries of Central America, logics and practices of elimination were also at work, whether due to combinations of the ideology of *mestizaje* combined with overt killing and repression, as in El Salvador in the 1930s, or *mestizaje* and geographic isolation, as with Afro-descendant and Indigenous groups on the Atlantic Coast that were largely shut out of the mestizo state in Honduras, Nicaragua, and Costa Rica. While all of these are generalizations, I outline them here to note that these dynamics are quite consistent with those under way in other settler states, including the United States.[26]

This matters because failing to understand the settler nature of these states leads us down the wrong path in terms of resisting their latest iteration, the neoliberal settler state. Recognizing how settler logics structured the frames of reference that continue to define the colonial exploitation in these countries is crucial to understanding the current moment and its implications for Indigenous peoples. Settler colonialism was the catalyst of capitalism's expansion and continues to structure life under capitalism as it has evolved. Capitalism's current iteration—neoliberalism—continues to be shaped by the settler-colonial imperative of dispossession, extraction, and elimination.

In the other half of what I characterized earlier as a dual theoretical elision, Indigenous studies theorists outside Latin America have tended to side-step an analysis of neoliberalism. This is so much the case that at a meeting several years ago to organize topics for the program of the Native American and Indigenous Studies Association, it was suggested by one participant that neoliberalism be removed from the list of topics because of its irrelevance. I argued that it should be retained because I knew it was likely to figure prominently in the panels and papers proposed by Indigenous scholars from Latin America. It was retained, but more as a democratic gesture than a recognition of its relevance for Indigenous peoples and a worthwhile area of study.[27] This exposes a dual theoretical gap in regard to state theorizations: theorizations of the settler state have not grappled fully enough with neoliberal capitalism, and theories of the neoliberal state fail to recognize the significance of settler logics that structure the conditions of state formation, including in its current iteration. This gap generally corresponds to the

North-South divide in the literature (northern Native American Studies heavily focused on the settler state; Indigenous studies south of the border focused on neoliberalism).

Neoliberalism, as an organizing logic and a set of practices and policies, has arguably been disastrous for everyone except the super-rich (Giroux 2011; Harvey 2007). But it brings a set of special concerns for Indigenous people. Neoliberalism can be understood as the extension of liberal ideas of free market economics that underpin modern capitalism, ideas that have enjoyed significant (though by no means complete) dominance since the mid-nineteenth century. The "neo" component is the late twentieth-century cumulative extension of competitive market principles to the entire social field, dictating government nonintervention not only in the economy, but in virtually every aspect of social life. Capital is shifted to the private sector and government is reduced, shrinking state social welfare programs and minimizing regulation of both social and economic interactions. Responsibility for mediating social inequality is devolved to civil society, spurring the growth of civil society organizing, NGOization, and the remaking of varied struggles for social justice into "rights struggles" waged exclusively on the legal terrain of the state. State divestment of the mediation of social inequality is a fundamental characteristic of the "cultural logics" of late capitalism, in Jameson's famous term (1992). In short, capitalism as an economic system by definition produces inequality. Harvey (2004) argues that neoliberalism engenders inequality through the uneven development of states and through the restructuring of class power in favor of the elites. It does so through the centralization of wealth and power in the hands of a few, achieved through dispossession of the public's wealth or land through privatization, shifts to financial markets as the base of the economy, the management and manipulation of crises, and state redistributions, particularly through tax codes that reward investment rather than wage earners. Harvey's term for this process is significant for us here: "accumulation by dispossession" (2004:64). Nuanced ethnographic readings of neoliberal capitalism's workings, such as that of Tsing (2015a), emphasize the complexities of local assemblages within capitalism. We might think of the multiplicity of interactions that these women's lives entail as they move through space in migration as such a local assemblage, through time and in different places, shedding light on the roles of race and gender in generative processes of the making and remaking of capitalism (see Tsing 2015b).

A fundamental component of neoliberalization in Latin America was the expansion of rights regimes and law as the primary field for state subject-making. For the shrinking state, governance would take place through investment in entrepreneurial citizenship (Postero 2006) and law and order, which necessitated new relationships to populations in processes of dispossession. In the United States as early as the 1970s, the state began to view trust relationships as overly burdensome and began to devolve sovereignty to the tribes, who then were made responsible for their own welfare, often with little preparation and few resources to do so (Biolsi 2007). In Mexico and Central America, by the early 1990s Indigenous people were recognized in constitutions for the first time and some measure of rights was accorded to them (Speed 2008b). While these seemed to be salutary processes and victories for peoples long in struggle, there were significant dangers associated with the incorporation of Indigenous peoples into the project of the neoliberal state. These particularly included the risks of reinscribing the power of the settler state through the laws and legal regimes that uphold it, as well as ceding a distinct status as collective Indigenous peoples different from other, individual-citizen minority populations.

However, as the women's stories will show us, unregulated neoliberalism is actually killing off its multiculturalist counterpart. It turns out that the fledgling rights regimes and legal structures long subordinated to executive power were unable to handle the task of managing the social outcomes of the free play of market forces. Unleashed from law and legality, markets bloom in a bloody Darwinian free-for-all of violence associated with the drugs, weapons, and human trafficking trades. The unfettered reign of private capital on a global scale also led to neoextractivist impulses that look remarkably similar to those at work in the initial stages of world colonization, bringing with them the intertwined mandates of dispossession and labor extraction. This extractivism takes the form not only of mining, but also of hydroelectric dams and tourism sites that extract value from the region through the ongoing process of dispossession and displacement. Not unlike the New Laws that fruitlessly mandated that wages be paid to workers in the *repartimiento*, the United Nations Declaration on the Rights of Indigenous Peoples now mandates that Indigenous peoples be "consulted" before their lands are dragged into these capitalist enterprises. Notably, those who protest are killed in extraordinary numbers[28] in an ongoing "get out of the way or die" logic of elimination. Racial logics continue to serve as the operational basis of capitalist exploitation, even in the ostensible "postracial" moment of neoliberal multiculturalism. States are enmeshed in this dynamic, implicated not just in a failure to stop it, but as active participants. In Mexico and Central America, violence is endemic and escalating. In the U.S. national security state, as we shall see, violations of rights as well as other violences are often perpetrated by the state, either through its policies or its agents. These dynamics all come together in the lives of Indigenous women migrants. In the chapters that follow, I will consider how settler structures and neoliberal dynamics produce the vulnerability of Indigenous women migrants, rendering them subject to multiple violences.

I begin in chapter 2 with three women's stories to explore the "home" community settings and the gendered forms of violence the women face, including domestic violence, community violence, gang violence, state violence, imperialist violence, and neoliberal violence. Next, in chapter 3, I delve into the women's journeys, considering how the current context of neoliberalism and the role particular manifestations of race, gender, and class play in Indigenous women's vulnerability to multiple social actors. This chapter brings in two new stories that expand our understanding of the intersectionality of violence and reveal how colonial tropes link with neoliberal logics to generate an astonishing lack of state accountability. In chapter 4, I turn to women's experience after crossing into the realm of the U.S. state. I consider immigration detention as part of a system of mass incarceration; the role that U.S. imperialism plays in punitive incarceration for Mexicans and Central Americans; the role of race, gender, and class in state interpellation; and the unique forms of violence to which Indigenous women are subject. In chapter 5, I then extend the stories of three women in order to analyze how women who are not detained or are postdetention are vulnerable to abusers ranging from domestic partners to human traffickers. Their stories render visible the neoliberal free market logics at work, and how these logics have contributed to the growth of intricate networks of violence in which U.S. and Latin American countries are enmeshed. Finally, in the conclusion, I draw together the arguments regarding the intersectional nature of violence against Indigenous women migrants and the fundamental place of the state in structuring that violence. I turn again to the enduring nature of settler structures and suggest that recent events in the United States reflect that permanence, as white supremacy, misogyny, and xenophobia have visibly and powerfully surged into view. I suggest that, long after neoliberalism has given way to some new phase of capitalist exploitation, settler tropes of race, gender, class, and belonging will continue to structure the conditions of possibility for women's lives and render them vulnerable in multiple ways.

CHAPTER TWO

Domestic Departures

Vulnerability in the Settler State

We sat together in the cold, unpleasant visitation room, leaning in to talk so that the friendly but vigilant CCA guard seated at the nearby table could not overhear our conversation. Turned sideways on the incongruous foam rubber chairs, Euphemia tapped her foot in the bright orange Croc shoes all women wear inside the Hutto facility. The jeans she had been given to wear were folded three times over at the bottom, far too long for her five-foot frame. She spoke softly but urgently, telling me how she had come to be here in this strange place. Her eyes filled with tears as she looked at the floor and her voice caught in her throat. "He hit me," she said, not looking up. "He hit me a lot." "I'm sorry," I said quietly, feeling the lack of appropriate words. "I'm so sorry you had to go through that." She looked up, now gazing intensely into my eyes, tears streaming down her face. "He wanted to kill me. He was going to kill me. I had to leave."

I had expected, in my long afternoons conversing with women in the cold and unfriendly visitation room, to hear stories of a difficult journey and the hardships of being incarcerated despite having committed no criminal offense. And I did hear those stories—captivating, terrible, compelling accounts of suffering and human resilience. What I did not expect, or certainly not at the level of frequency with which I heard them, were the seemingly endemic stories of domestic violence. After three years of visiting women in Hutto and two years of recording the oral histories of Indigenous and non-Indigenous migrant women, I can count on one hand the number who did not experience domestic violence. Not everyone came because they were fleeing domestic violence, but often even women fleeing other threats had experiences of intrafamilial violence. It became clear to me, early on, that intrafamilial violence was something that virtually every woman encountered and that marked every woman's life in important ways.

I was not particularly comfortable with the issue. As a Native woman and a researcher and activist working with Indigenous women in Mexico for the last twenty years, I have certainly been aware that domestic violence is a major problem affecting Indigenous and Native women everywhere. But I always sidestepped the topic, tending to focus instead on state-perpetrated gender violence. Though violence among family members and loved ones is indeed abhorrent, my discomfort was not due to any repulsion I felt. Rather, I suffered from what Veena Das has called "definitional vertigo" around the term *violence* (2008:283). I knew that, in spite of the abundance of individually pathologizing literature, domestic violence is intimately bound up with other forms of violence, but I did not know how to talk about the intersections coherently. How is the violence associated with neoliberal multicriminalism—gang violence, drug violence, militarization, and state violence—related to intrafamilial violence, which is so easily relegated to the "private" sphere?

Feminist theories about gender violence often rely on the concept of a continuum of violence, which emphasizes that all forms of gender violence, from intrapersonal to wartime mass-scale rape, are products of dominant patriarchal ideologies that are deeply misogynistic (Kelly 1987; Sev'er 1999). The continuum-of-violence theory, in its best iterations, moves us past distinctions between the public and the private spheres as relevant for understanding gender violence (Cockburn 2004; Giles and Hyndman 2004; Moser 2001). However, the continuum model tends to recommit the age-old feminist error of grouping all women together and not accounting for the ways that other aspects of women's lives—such as race, class, and immigration or disability status—render some women more vulnerable than others. How does the continuum account for the fact that Indigenous women are more likely than other women in society to be victims of gender violence?

Intersectionality theory (Collins 1998; Crenshaw 1991) analyzes the ways that hierarchies of power exist along multiple socially defined axes, such as race, class, gender, and national origin, and the ways that these categories "mutually construct each other via structural inequalities and social interaction, creating a matrix of intersecting hierarchies that is not merely additive but multiplicative in terms of unearned privilege, domination, and oppression" (Erez, Adelman, and Gregory 2009:34). Intersectional analyses have made it indisputably clear that these different axes of oppression are not only interrelated but mutually constitutive—and thus, one cannot understand an Indigenous woman's oppression simply by considering her gender. Likewise, one cannot understand an Indigenous woman's experience of gender violence by considering only her gender.

A related concern with the continuum model is that it tends to conceptualize different types of violence as discrete forms located along the continuum—although in the same category of misogyny-inspired actions, each is, definitionally speaking, a recognizably distinct practice. This obscures the mutually constituted nature of most gender violence. For example, domestic violence is in part generated by state violence (Bourgois 2001). As the stories examined in this chapter show, the violence (often but not necessarily gendered) unleashed during wartime or counterinsurgency leaves in its wake emotional damage that may be acted out through the perpetuation of violence against family members (see Wing 1996 for an analysis of this process in Palestine and South Africa). However, the continuum locates the interpersonal and the state-sponsored at opposite ends of the spectrum, limiting our ability to understand their relationship.

The constant presence and inevitability of the domestic violence in the detained women's stories has forced me to try to come to terms with the difficult nature of the relationship between this and other forms of violence as they play out at the intersection of various axes of oppression. Intersectionality theory helped a great deal in this regard. Indeed, as Crenshaw wrote in her seminal essay on intersectionality of women of color in women's shelters in minority communities in Los Angeles

> in most cases, the physical assault that leads women to these shelters is merely the most immediate manifestation of the subordination they experience. Many women who seek protection are unemployed or underemployed, and a good number of them are poor. Shelters serving these women cannot afford to address only the violence inflicted by the batterer; they must also confront the other multilayered and routinized forms of domination that often converge in these women's lives, hindering their ability to create alternatives to the abusive relationships that brought them to shelters in the first place. Many women of color, for example, are burdened by poverty, childcare responsibilities, and the lack of job skills. These burdens, largely the consequence of gender and class oppression, are then compounded by the racially discriminatory employment and housing practices women of color often face, as well as by the disproportionately high unemployment among people of color that makes battered women of color less able to depend on the support of friends and relatives for temporary shelter. (1991:1246)

While Crenshaw was obviously talking about a different demographic and geographic space, the argument about structural violence could be virtually transposed to a discussion of Indigenous women. That is, undoubtedly for many Indigenous women migrants, the domestic violence that leads them to migrate is merely the most immediate manifestation of the subordination they experience. Many Indigenous women who migrate are unemployed or underemployed, and most of them are poor. They also confront other multilayered and routinized forms of domination that converge in their lives, hindering their ability to create alternatives to the abusive relationships that forced them to migrate in the first place. Many Indigenous women migrants, for example, are burdened by poverty, childcare responsibilities, and a lack of job skills. These dynamics, largely the consequence of gender and class oppression, are compounded by the racially discriminatory practices in social welfare, health, and administration of justice. All this combines with extraordinary levels of impunity, resulting in a situation in which poor, Indigenous women are unlikely to ever gain protection or justice from agents of the state, and in addition, the U.S. national security state and its policies of "prevention by deterrence," mean they cannot gain shelter and are likely to have their rights violated again in the foreign state where they have sought refuge. Crenshaw's argument about structural intersectionality is clearly demonstrated in these women's lives; what I have found is that the women's stories themselves revealed those intersections with great clarity. In this chapter, through an examination of the domestic violence stories of three women, I will analyze the multilayered, interrelated, and mutually constitutive nature of the myriad forms of violence suffered by Indigenous women migrants. My purpose is to demonstrate the interrelatedness of the forms of violence they suffer, and particularly the ways that state violence gives shape to other violences that Indigenous women suffer. I will argue that it is their location at the intersection of these axes of oppression that renders Indigenous women particularly vulnerable, and that this vulnerability is a direct result of settler ideologies.

Intrafamilial Violence

Euphemia's story, like that of Ysinia, reflects multilayered and intersectional violence. Both of their journeys began with domestic violence perpetrated by their male partners:

> Euphemia's husband—like Euphemia, a Chol Maya from Chiapas, Mexico— beat her with increasing frequency and intensity over the course of their nineteen-year relationship. When they first began living together, her mother-in-law, in whose house they lived for the first several years, encouraged him to hit Euphemia to "teach her how to be a good wife." Still, he did not regularly hit her until several years later, when she lost their only child

well into her pregnancy, a loss she attributed to the difficult conditions of the refugee camp they lived in for a short period while displaced from their town by paramilitary violence. He blamed her for the loss and grew increasingly frustrated that she did not become pregnant again. He began to be jealous, accusing her of sleeping around and using plant-based remedies to prevent pregnancy. This went on for several years before he began a relationship with another woman, who bore him three children over the next decade. However, he continued to hold Euphemia as his wife and demand that she perform a "wife's duties," which included having intercourse with him. Euphemia did not try to end the relationship because as a woman alone, with no land, she would have few options for survival. She once asked the community authorities to intervene to stop his abuse, but in the mediation they called, the authorities seemed to believe that the problem was largely that she was jealous of the other wife, and they instructed him only that it remained his duty to continue to support her. They also instructed her to continue to be a good wife and serve her husband.

Eventually, because of conflicts between political factions within the community, Euphemia's husband told her that they were leaving for the nearby town of Ocosingo. She lived with him in a rented room there for some time, possibly two years, and over that time she became increasingly afraid. He was secretive about his activities and would fly into a rage if she asked him anything at all about where he went, even though he was sometimes gone for several days at a time. Euphemia took in wash and sold eggs for a small income, but her husband did not want her to go out for work. He threatened to kill her if she left the house for any reason other than to buy groceries at the small market nearby. She was a virtual hostage but felt she had nowhere to turn. She finally made her escape when he beat her so severely she was knocked unconscious and a neighbor took her to the hospital. Terrified that he would come for her, she left the hospital and took public transportation to the state capital, Tuxtla Gutierrez. She had been in Tuxtla for about a year when she ran into a couple from her home community who told her that her husband was looking for her. Afraid that he would find her and that this couple might even tell him where she was, she made the decision to flee to the United States.

Euphemia and Ysinia are not alone in having fled domestic violence by journeying to the United States. Though we do not have access to data about how many of the asylum claims in the Hutto facility are "gender-based claims," women's oral reports suggest it is a significant number. Many women report that they are fleeing violence by a domestic partner or other family member. By no means simply a "private" matter, this type of violence is one component of a multilayered social dynamic in which ideologies of race and class interact with gender in particular ways to define women's vulnerability to violence. The women's stories render this intersectional dynamic visible, and also reveal how different forms of violence are mutually constitutive. In particular, we can see the traces of state violence and how they give rise to and define the conditions for domestic violence. But before turning to a full analysis, I want to share another woman's story that lends further complexity to these points.

Marisol was born in the Ixcan, Guatemala. She does not know how she came to live with adoptive parents in Campeche, Mexico. She did not question the fact that she was brown skinned, while they were tall and fair, until many years later. When she was fourteen, her adoptive mother told a family friend that he could marry her. Marisol refused, and the man proceeded to sexually assault her on several occasions, apparently with her mother's consent. Furious at Marisol's stubborn refusal to obey her demand, her mother told her, "What do you think? That with your face a prince is going to arrive for you?" Then one night she awoke to a strange man in her room, clearly intending to rape her. He told her she had to submit, as he had paid her mother money in exchange for sex with her. Marisol managed to escape the man and fled her house. At that point, she decided her only choice was to go and live with the man who wanted to marry her, as she could not return home and had nowhere else to go. She lived with him for a number of months but never adjusted. He would beat her if she cried or refused to have sex, and he forbade her to visit her siblings.

Eventually, she fled after a harsher-than-usual beating and approached her father. Seeing how she had been treated, he brought her back into the family home, where she lived, in a great deal of tension with her mother, until she met and married a man of her own choosing. He was a good provider, but shortly after they married he began to express jealousy about the man she had been with previously, telling her, "I love you. But you should have waited for me." He would fly into rages, especially when drinking, and beat her. She had two children by him and endured his beatings for seven years before leaving him.

A few years later, while working alone in a shop, Marisol was attacked by a local man known to have carried out several previous rapes, about which the police had done nothing. After brutally raping her, he began calmly putting on his pants. Something about his casual attitude caused Marisol to snap, and she grabbed a machete, whacking him with it once in the back and once in the leg.

Terrified, Marisol fled the town. She was certain that the man would go to the police, who would almost certainly not arrest him for the rape but rather arrest her for the machetazos (machete blows). She called a family member and borrowed money, departing that same afternoon for the border of the United States.

Settler Tropes and Genocidal Moments

The gendered and sexual violence that these women experienced, while individual and carried out through intrafamilial relationships, is nevertheless a product of larger structures of power, particularly state power. Gender and sexuality have been and remain key tools in the settler-state toolbox. As Andrea Smith has argued, "It has been through sexual violence and through the imposition of European gender relationships on Native communities that Europeans were able to colonize Native peoples" (2005:139). Huhndorf and Suzack also outline the gendered and violent nature of colonization: "For indigenous women, colonization has involved their removal from positions of power, the replacement of traditional gender roles with Western patriarchal practices, the exertion of colonial control over indigenous communities, through the management of women's bodies, and sexual violence" (2010:1). The gendered violence of colonization was constitutive of the modern settler state.

This is true both in terms of direct physical violence (as Smith refers to in the foregoing quote) and in terms of the ideologies deployed to justify the violence of dispossession. Morgensen (2010:106), following Stoler (1995), theorizes how "colonial biopolitics" employs gender and sexuality to discursively construct the primitive and disappearing Indian and physically regulate and maintain control over those who remain. Indeed, as Morgensen shows, "colonists interpreted diverse practices of gender and sexuality as signs of a general primitivity among Native peoples. Over time, they produced a colonial necropolitics that framed Native peoples as queer populations marked for death" (2010:106). Razack (2015) has also explored the ways that the narrative trope of the primitive and disappearing Indian underpins the settler-colonial violence waged against them, and specifically how it interlocks with gendered versions of the rapeable Indian woman to feed both violence against them and impunity for it. Indeed, the ideological construction of Indigenous women as violatable has underpinned genocidal policies against Indigenous peoples from colonial through modern state times (Razack 2015; A. Smith 2005). As Audra Simpson writes in "The

State Is a Man," "Indian women 'disappear' because they have been deemed killable, rapeable, expendable. Their bodies have historically been rendered less valuable because of what they are taken to represent: land, reproduction, Indigenous kinship and governance, an alternative to heteropatriarchal and Victorian rules of descent" (2016:10). Settler ideologies of gender and race thus construct Indigenous women as the inevitable subjects of sexual violence and control.

If, as Veracini (2013a) argues, the end goal of settler colonialism is the elimination of the Indigenous population, reaching success when it has reduced the population to a manageable remnant, then undoubtedly, imposed gender norms and sexual violence have played a key role in both the reduction of the population and the subordination and control of the surviving "remnant."[1] Because settler colonialism as a structure and logic is ongoing, gender and sexual violence remain crucial to the colonial process, and, as Razack states, "the imprinting of colonial power on both Indigenous men and women continues apace and in gendered ways" (2015:22). Ideological construction of Indigenous women as objects of sexual and gendered control is fundamental to understanding both the violence against them—including domestic violence—and the near total impunity for it (Deer 2005). Their vulnerability reinforces the settler logic of the disappearing Indian marked for death, a logic that remains operative today. Estrella's story will help elucidate the point.

Estrella, a Maya Mam woman from San Marcos, Guatemala, fled an uncle who had killed her father on the family patio over a land dispute. I met the nineteen-year-old while she was detained at Hutto. With a slight four-foot-eleven frame, she spoke softly in halting Spanish and often appeared on the verge of tears. Slowly, as I visited her regularly through the Hutto Visitation Project, she began to tell me her story. After her father's death, the uncle—her father's sister's husband—began beating her and raping her, eventually leaving her pregnant. He was sick, she explained, and drank heavily because he had had terrible experiences during La Violencia (The Violence), Guatemala's thirty-six-year civil war. Estrella fled when her child was two months old, after repeated attempts to get the police to intervene went nowhere. Her journey to the United States was harrowing. She traveled in the company of several other migrants from Guatemala City who were fleeing gang extortion and death threats. These male companions protected her, she said, when two Maras (shorthand for youth gang members), who had boarded the train on which they were riding threatened to rape her. She eventually reached the border, only to be abducted by cartel gangs in Reynosa. With her limited Spanish, she struggled to understand the demands that she call someone to obtain a ransom for her release. In any case, she had no one to call and was detained for at least a week before she was beaten, threatened, and finally released. She turned herself in to the U.S. Border Patrol, believing she had reached safety. When she expressed fear of being returned to her country, she was sent into the immigration detention system to await her fate as an asylum seeker. She had already been detained for months when I met her, and her detention dragged on as the asylum office "looked for" a Mam interpreter. I watched as her emotional state, not good to begin with, declined week by week as she waited and waited, spending idle hours worrying about the infant daughter she had left behind and fearing that she would be returned to Guatemala. Finally, after a year in detention, she was so desperate to get out of Hutto, she nearly took voluntary departure. But a sympathetic immigration judge, noting the strength of her case, set her free without bond.

Estrella is clear about the relationship between the violence she has suffered and the state-generated violence of the civil war. That war itself must be understood as settler-state violence. In any settler context, there are moments of rupture when settler policies and practices of management erupt into more openly genocidal approaches, what Razack refers to as "genocidal moments" when control of the still-present Native population is in question. In these specific modern histories of state-sponsored genocidal violence, the settler trope of the violatable Indian woman is openly wielded to carry out and justify the violence that women experience.

There is perhaps no better example of this than Guatemala. The country's five centuries of colonial history have been profoundly marked by racialized dispossession and labor extraction. Colonization "disrupted Indigenous people's way of life and limited their access to land and productive labor, forcing seasonal migration and slave labor conditions for entire families" (Crosby and Lykes 2011:460). Gomez and Picq (2017) argue that land demarcation was a key tool of state making. In 1871 Guatemala created the first national Registry of Property and required that land titles be registered with the state as private property. Indigenous peoples who sought to protect their land titles by registering them were forced to give up communal land titles and accept private ones (Gomez and Picq 2017). Gomez and Picq note the similarity to settler strategies in other places: "The Registry transformed Maya territories into private property in a settler logic of dispossession similar to the 1887 General Allotment Act that permitted the US government to divide native territory into individual allotments" (2017:793). Naturally, as in other settler states, the Guatemalan state declared unclaimed lands "vacant" and "unproductive" and seized them for itself.

Racialization was complex in Guatemala. On the one hand, the state worked through local governments to eliminate the Indigenous population by declaring them "*Ladino*" (essentially the equivalent of *mestizo*, meaning "mixed race").[2] As in Mexico and other parts of Central America, the idea that miscegenation could render Indians part of the nation-state and eliminate them as a (land-bearing) problem tied into larger discourses of eugenics and social Darwinism circulating in the Western world at the time. However, in spite of these "whitening decrees" (Castro and Picq 2017), white European settlers remained highly segregated from the majority-Indigenous population in an intensely hierarchical relationship (Rodriguez and Menjívar 2015). Eight elite extended Guatemalan families are said to control 75 percent of the country's wealth to the present day (Fuentes Knight 2011; see Casaus Arzú 1995 for an analysis of the significance of family networks in racialized power in Guatemala). In contrast to other parts of Mesoamerica (and the United States), assimilation was never a settler strategy in Guatemala, and a strict racial separation enforced European settler power. As Crosby and Lykes argue, this process was also "profoundly gendered and sexualized, with indigenous women experiencing particular forms of violence and exclusion" (2011:460).

In the mid-twentieth century, the assimilation was tried again under the government of Jacobo Arbenz. The 1944 revolution that allowed him to assume power also led to a strongly progressive government that sought better conditions for workers, peasants, students, and the urban poor, including social and political reforms as well as agrarian reform. Yet, like other liberal governments of the era, particularly that of Mexico, the Arbenz government pursued indigenist policies of assimilation for Indigenous peoples, believing that it was in their best interest for them to modernize and become full citizens of the nation-state (Hale 2006). The Arbenz government discursively invoked nationalism and the notion of a unified nation under a banner of "*Somos todos guatemaltecos*" (We are all Guatemalans) (Castro and Picq 2017). In 1945 the National Indigenist Institute was created to facilitate this process. Like other such institutes in Latin America (Mexico's was created in 1948), its goal was to solve the "Indian problem" through assimilation and modernization.[3] According to Castro and Picq (2017), during this period the government called on Indigenous authorities to turn in communal land titles and dismantled Indigenous municipalities in pursuit of a "homogeneous nationality," reflecting a settler impulse toward dispossession and erasure.

The Arbenz government provoked settler anxieties by threatening to undermine elite settler control. Class conflict quickly arose as elites violently opposed land claims by Indigenous peasants. The government of "eternal spring" also provoked anxieties abroad. The United States, interpreting its socialist orientation as a communist threat, took out the Arbenz government in a CIA-backed coup in 1954 (Schlesinger and Kinzer 1990). The years following the coup would see the emergence of guerrilla organizing, provoking further elite anxieties in which the ostensible communist threat combined with fears of Maya organizing and involvement with the guerrilla forces. Hale refers to this period, roughly from 1954 to the mid-1970s, as "the golden era of ladino dominance" (2006:48). He argues that while Guatemalan society returned to its harsh racial status quo of "separate and unequal" following the coup, a curious dichotomy emerged in terms of the state, which maintained a somewhat assimilationist bent, what Hale terms "disciplinary assimilation," under policies that went under various names, such as integrationism and development (Hale 2006:48).[4]

By the mid-1970s, these anxieties motivated the Guatemalan state to launch a genocidal "moment" waged directly by military and paramilitary forces trained, funded, and supervised by the United States in scorched-earth campaigns, that included forced torture and disappearance, civil patrols, and sexual violence and slavery. More than two hundred thousand people were killed, about 83 percent of them Maya, according to a report by the UN-backed Commission for Historical Clarification (1999). The report also concluded that the vast majority—93 percent—of human rights violations perpetrated during the conflict were carried out by state forces and military groups. During this period, referred to simply as "La Violencia," women were subjected to rape and gendered violence on a massive scale (Hastings 2002; Sanford 2008). Irma Alicia Velasquez Nimatuj, a Maya K'iche anthropologist and journalist who produced an exhaustive expert report on the sexual violence, argues that "forces used sexual violence as part of their counterinsurgency strategy of destroying an imagined 'internal enemy,' embodied largely by Indigenous communities. In the context of counterinsurgency, the state saw indigenous women as the mothers of future guerrillas and thus a necessary enemy to destroy" (Velasquez Nimatuj 2016:4). It is estimated that one hundred thousand women were raped. The vast majority of these crimes were never prosecuted.[5]

The extreme gendered and genocidal violence of La Violencia was not magically washed away with the end of the armed conflict in 1995. As Victoria Sanford has argued, "It is against this backdrop of genocide and impunity that Guatemalans today find themselves living in an extremely violent country" (2008:104). Sanford examines the relationship between discourses and practices of past violence and those of current violence against women and demonstrates strong connections between them, a "particular lexicon that we can trace from the 1980s to the present" (2008:119). I suggest that this is a settler-generated lexicon that has existed and been mobilized against Indigenous peoples through gendered violence over the course of several centuries.

In *Los tejidos que lleva el alma: Memoria de las mujeres mayas sobrevivientes de la violación sexual durante el conflicto armado* (*The weavings the soul carries: Memory of Mayan women survivors of rape during the armed conflict*) (Equipo de Estudios Comunitaros y Acción Psicosocial and Union Nacional de Mujeres Guatemaltecas 2011), Mayan women survivors, working with a group of social psychologists, put forward an analysis of the sexual violence carried out during the armed conflict. One of the interesting aspects of their analysis is that gendered control of women's bodies and women's sexuality was endemic before the armed conflict. Rape was also a common occurrence. They locate the start of these forms of oppression in colonialism and emphasize their endurance through the centuries and trace their evolution. For example, they discuss how large landowners regularly regarded Indigenous women working for them as their property and as avaliable for their use, including their sexual use. They note how this evolved through time, with Ladino families condoning or even encouraging their sons to "use" the domestic staff in order to limit their excesses outside the home. They elaborate on how these forms of masculine control were also the norm in their communities before the war, noting that rape within marriage and within the community was common. They write, "It is important to highlight that the gender violence is immersed in the socioeconomic and political context of Guatemala, and it is as much a manifestation of, as a result, of inherent power relations existing between women and men. This violence is founded in all of the social structures where male power predominates, including the state when it exercises hierarchical and patriarchal control. While this violence is structural, the context of the armed conflict took it further" (2011:152–53, translation mine). Their analysis leaves no doubt that colonially structured gender norms and racialization created patterns of gender violence that fed the gendered violence of the war.

At the same time, the gendered violence of the war feeds gender violence in the postconflict period. These dynamics emerge in the women's stories—such as Estrella's attributing her uncle's alcoholism and violence to his experiences during the war—and are a recurring theme in oral histories from Guatemala. While we do not know exactly how Marisol ended up with a family of *güeros* (white people) in Campeche, her age (about thirty when I met her in 2011) makes it likely that she and her birth family were displaced and affected by the violence of the war, which raged in the Ixcan in the early 1980s. Thousands fled Guatemala for Mexico, mostly to refugee camps in Chiapas, Quintana Roo, and Campeche (Manz 1988). Her adoption into this family set up the conditions that allowed racialized and gendered violence to be perpetrated against her. Their stories reflect what Veena Das has referred to as the centrality of gender for "understanding what connects the national to the domestic" and "the deep connections between the spectacular and the everyday" (2008:283). The domestic circumstances Marisol faced that facilitated the violence against her cannot be separated from the "spectacular" national violence of La Violencia, which in fact generated it, nor can the trauma Estrella experienced at the hands of her uncle, as she herself acknowledged. Thus, state violence cannot be extricated from other forms of violence because it is state discourse and practice that set the context and generate the conditions in which such violence can be enacted.

In Mexico, the settler state also deployed highly gendered patriarchal tropes of Indigenous rapeability, though these played out somewhat differently than in Guatemala as a result of gender's conjunction with race. Unlike Guatemala's racial apartheid, in Mexico the myth of *mestizaje* worked to discursively erase living Indigenous people, rendering them a part of the country's historic past and racial mix, but not part of its present population, effectively occluding the largest Indigenous population of any country in the Americas. Meanwhile, as in Guatemala, in the twentieth century the state and its indigenist anthropologists worked to eliminate the Indigenous population through "modernization." Discursively constructing this population as backward and uncivilized, the state sought to bring them into modern society through the elimination of Indigenous languages, dress, and forms of living. These strategies erupted as openly genocidal moments only when Indigenous people made themselves unavoidably present, most notably in the 1994 Zapatista uprising. So successfully hegemonic was the discourse of *mes-*

tizaje in Mexico that when the largely Mayan uprising began in 1994, people in many areas of the country were shocked, not at the Indians' bold resistance, but at the fact that they existed at all. The state's genocidal response was a counterinsurgency campaign lasting more than a decade, in which the state fomented paramilitary violence and deployed highly gendered forms of violence, most notable in the massacre at Acteal in 1997 (R. A. Hernández 1998).

Mexico remains a highly racialized society, with phenotype closely tied to social class and privilege. Yet the workings of race in this settler context are obscured by the master narrative of *mestizaje*, which holds that racially the country is all one "cosmic race."[6] While assimilation played a key role in Mexico, as in the United States and elsewhere, the "invisibilizing" of living Indigenous people through *mestizaje* meant that the only acknowledged Indigenous people were those who were highly visible. In essence, the state constructed Indianness as the presence of readily identifiable features such as Indigenous language and dress. Descent is largely irrelevant in the schema developed by the Mexican state. This provides a fluidity—the ability to "stop being Indian" at any time by dropping the language and dress.[7] The settler logics of elimination are at work in this construction, which (combined with overt policies of deculturalization and widespread racial discrimination) serve to push Indigenous people toward deidentification.

The complex question of race and Indigeneity in Mexico is often reflected in the stories of Indigenous women migrants. For example, Marisol's mother's comment about "her face not bringing her a prince" likely referenced her phenotype and its implications for her place in the racialized social hierarchy in Mexico, in which whites are dominant and Indians at the bottom. In trying to compel Marisol to submit to her demands that she marry, her mother deployed this racial trope to invoke her position of dominance over Marisol. The gender violence she experienced is ideologically justified by deploying race and class. Race magnifies the vulnerability of Indigenous women to violence, locating them in a social structure in which they are understood to be subordinate and violatable. Yet race fluidity and class also play important roles. Marisol, as the adopted daughter of a white Campechano family and lacking the requisite language and dress, would not be interpellated by most people as Indigenous. When fleeing, she was able to quickly turn to a relative and get sufficient money to take a first-class bus to the border, freeing her of the hardships many others experience. These advantages, while not eliminating all the hardships of migrating by any means, do reduce vulnerability and reflect important class differences in women's migration experiences. In these dynamics, we see how race and class intersect with gender, creating the particular context in which such violence is generated and accepted.

The Current Context: From Impunity to Feminicide

As we can see from the foregoing discussion, settler ideologies of race and gender manifest differently across space and time, but they take on particular relevance in the lawlessness of the current moment (discussed at more length in chapter 4). Perpetrators' near total lack of accountability for gender violence is present throughout the women's stories. For example, Euphemia's community authorities completely sidestepped an acknowledgment of the violence being perpetrated against her. Notable in Marisol's story was her understanding that the police would never detain her rapist but would come after her for having responded to it. Estrella also fled after repeatedly trying to get the police to help her, to no avail. Gender violence is rarely investigated or punished in Mexico, Guatemala, or Honduras, and less so when the victim is an Indigenous woman.

So intensified is this impunity at the current juncture that it has given rise to the phenomenon of feminicide. Over the last two decades, tens of thousands of women have been violently murdered, often sexually assaulted, tortured, sometimes dismembered, and tossed out into streets, fields, and garbage piles like so much waste. The phenomenon of woman killing was first named *feminicide* in Juarez, Mexico, in the mid-1990s, but the term was soon being applied throughout Mexico and Central America as the murders of women racheted up.

Analysts endeavoring to understand feminicide have had to come to terms with the fact that the violence could not be attributable to a single serial killer or a particular cartel, or even the increase in drug trafficking more generally (with its correlated rise in murders overall). Instead, the thousands upon thousands of murdered women are products of a much broader and more heinous social dynamic, with perpetrators spread throughout the social fabric (Fregoso and Bejarano 2010a). In other words, women are being killed by everyone, from cartels and gangs to legal authorities, from strangers to husbands, fathers, and brothers. Grasping this, of course, necessitates recognizing the interrelatedness of various forms of violence. Although some feminicide analyses have focused so heavily on gender—women are being killed precisely (or only) because they are women—that they have neglected to incorporate race and class, a few put them usefully in the forefront

(Olivera 2010; Weissman 2009). This is important because while women are killed because they are women, poor and Indigenous women are more likely to be subject to feminicidal violence than others.

Also importantly, scholars working on feminicide have highlighted the role of the state in setting the conditions under which multiple, interrelated forms of gender violence are generated and tolerated (Domínguez Rubalcava and Ravelo Blancas 2010; Sanford 2008). Fregoso and Bejarano (2010a) convincingly argue that in Mexico, the state's failure to hold anyone accountable for the mass-scale violence against women not only facilitates but also *generates* further violence, as Sanford (2008) argues regarding Guatemala. It is crucial to locate "domestic" violence of the kind experienced by Ysinia, Estrella, Marisol, and Eugenia within the broader panorama of feminicide because, as analysts of gender violence have noted, formulating violence against women as a purely interpersonal phenomenon only serves to depoliticize gender violence (Godoy-Paiz 2008; Menjívar 2012; Price 2012), effectively letting the state off the hook.

IN THIS CHAPTER, I have taken Euphemia's, Marisol's, and Estrella's stories as evidence not only that the multiple forms of violence they are subject to are gendered, but also that race and class intersect with gender in ways that cannot be ignored. Further, I have argued that all forms of violence are interrelated and mutually constitutive. Individual or interpersonal gender violence cannot be understood outside the historical and ideological structures that give rise to it and in which it is enacted. If we want to understand violence in all of its social depth and complexity, we must take the interaction of all of these social forms into account. I have argued elsewhere that we should think about gender violence not so much as a continuum — in which separate forms of violence succeed each other along a line moving from individual and interpersonal to mass scale and state sponsored — but rather as a kind of mosaic, in which many distinct forms are brought together and the overall picture created by their juxtaposition can only be fully comprehended by contemplating them all together (Speed 2014).

As I have argued here, these dynamics of violence are profoundly rooted in the settler state and its logics of elimination, with racial and gender ideologies that, while playing out differently over time and space and in distinct national contexts, nevertheless fundamentally structure the social field in which Indigenous women's lives unfold. It is their location at the intersection of these axes of oppression that renders Indigenous women particularly vulnerable, and this vulnerability is a direct result of settler ideologies.

Further, specific histories of how settler logics have unfolded as racialized and gendered state violence and the current state-defined context of a particularly vicious and unrestrained capitalism (discussed further in chapter 4) set the ideological and material conditions for the violence women experience. In this sense, domestic violence fits into a larger picture of ongoing settler elimination and vulnerability to disappearance. Thus vulnerability, far from being an inherent state or characteristic of the women themselves, is rather a structural condition imposed on them.

CHAPTER THREE

Perilous Passages
The Neoliberal Multicriminal Settler State

Virgilia departed her home in southern Mexico, fleeing a domestic partner who had been beating her for years, breaking her clavicle twice and leaving permanent scars on her face and back. A Tzotzil speaker from the highlands of Chiapas, she had been living in the city of San Cristobal de Las Casas since she was fourteen, when she left her community to become a live-in domestic servant in the home of a Ladino family. One of her main motivations in leaving her community was to escape her father, who drank heavily and had been physically abusive to her, as well as to her mother and siblings. She formed a relationship with a man, also a Tzotzil speaker, when she was seventeen. He soon became abusive. She had two children with her partner, ages four and seven when she fled, whom she left in the care of her sister. The decision to leave her children "broke her heart," she told me, but she was certain that it was only a matter of time before her partner, who had become involved in illegal smuggling activity and regularly carried weapons, would kill her, leaving her children with no one to support them. She paid a coyote $3,000 to bring her north, most of it borrowed from her sister and the family she worked for.

The journey was perilous. Although she had lived in the town of San Cristobal, twenty-five-year-old Virgilia was not worldly. The life of Indigenous women in domestic work in San Cristobal, a city of about 185,000 at the time, is highly circumscribed, and their activities are often largely constrained to their homes, their places of work, and the market. Her Spanish remained limited. She was terrified throughout the journey, she told me. There was good reason to be afraid. She and others were stranded for days — eventually without food and water — when the train they were riding broke down in a remote area. A man who offered her and two others shelter in his house threatened to rape her in the middle of the night. She was held for ransom for a number of days by drug cartels in Reynosa, during which time she was sexually assaulted. She was freed after a brother living in Oklahoma City paid the ransom. She then spent days — she is unsure how many — in the desert after crossing the border, and she was abandoned by her pollero[1] when the U.S. Border Patrol approached and she could not run fast enough to stay with the group. He shouted, "Córrele pinche india! Apúrate!" (roughly, "Run, damned Indian! Hurry up!") as he ran off. Virgilia was apprehended and taken into Border Patrol custody.

As the stories of Ysinia, Euphemia, Marisol, Estrella, and Virgilia reflect, Indigenous women migrants from Mexico and Central America to the United States suffer human rights violations at every step, especially on the perilous passage through Mexico, with its veritable gauntlet of dangers. Their stories tell us that women do not make the decision to depart home and family and undertake an unsafe journey to an unknown future lightly. Whether they are fleeing domestic violence, gang violence, cartel threats, economic violence, or some conjunction of these, migrating is a serious and brave undertaking that women invariably describe as their only option. In the previous chapter, I examined the violence that compels women to leave home, particularly the domestic or intrafamilial violence that marks so many women's lives. In this chapter, I turn to the journeys they undertake to examine how the same structures of power that rendered them vulnerable to violence at home render them vulnerable in new ways once they have fled.

Exploring these questions through the lens of the journeys of Indigenous women migrants is of particular relevance as Indigenous migration out of Mexico and Central America is on the rise, in large part because of the dynamics discussed in this chapter. Even as Mexican migration in general has slowed in recent years (Terrazas 2010), Indigenous migration has increased, making up a larger portion of total migration than ever before. It is estimated that in the United States there are currently as many as 1,250,000 Latin American immigrants whose native language is not Spanish (Hispanic Economics n.d.), and for these Indigenous migrants, the dangerous journey from their home countries is even more risky, life in the United States even more difficult, and immigration detention even more isolating and frightening than it is for others. Vogt (2013) has called for analysts to take the liminal spaces of the migration route seriously and to understand migration experiences along that route as inscribed within larger structures of power. Here, I consider how Indigenous women, in particular, experience the liminal spaces of the migrant route and are rendered vulnerable in a multiplicity of ways by an array of potential threats presented by overarching structures of power in the neoliberal multicriminal settler state. Departing from the stories of the women we got to know in chapter 2, this chapter brings in new stories and builds on the previous discussion by expanding our understanding of the intersectionality of violence and rendering visible how colonial tropes intersect with neoliberal logics to generate an astonishing lack of state accountability not only in Honduras, Guatemala, and Mexico, but in the United States as well. I will argue that as neoliberalizing states abandon their populations to market forces, sending Indigenous people into ever-increasing levels of poverty and marginalization, those same market forces redefine the state itself. In that context, violence and lack of accountability are not simply matters of criminal elements and corruption, but rather structural features of the neoliberal multicriminal settler state.

Socially Organized Violence: From Narco Gangs to Agents of the State

While histories of state violence are evident in the women's stories as formative factors of domestic and other violence, the determinative role of current state policies, ideologies, and actions is also visible. Neoliberalism took hold of countries like Guatemala, Honduras, and Mexico in the late 1980s and early 1990s, as the U.S. model of unrestrained capitalism swept throughout the hemisphere. In what was viewed at the time as the inevitable march of "globalization," the idea that states should reduce social spending and remove all barriers to the (ostensibly) free flow of capital through the economy was enshrined in reformed constitutions in many countries of Latin America: trade barriers were lifted; resources, industry, and finance sectors privatized; and collectively held lands parceled out and rendered newly alienable. Governments were to restrain themselves from any intervention in the economy and the mediation of social inequality would be left to the play of market forces. Indeed, what characterizes neoliberal states, as Gledhill has pointed out, is the "elision of the distinction between a market *economy* and a market *society*, to the point where the latter seems to engulf life itself" (2005:340). Indeed.

As discussed in chapter 1, the process of neoliberalization was supposed to bring democracy and rule of law with it. It was assumed that free market capitalism, democracy, and respect for human rights went hand in hand, including the recognition of the rights of Indigenous people often included in these reforms, and there were faltering steps in that direction (Speed 2008b). However, it was not long before neoliberalism's extreme market logics combined with the preexisting dynamics of crime, corruption, and impunity to unleash a new status quo in which the only law that matters is the law of supply and demand, and the only logic is that of the profit motive. Under this system, which I have referred to elsewhere as neoliberal multicriminalism

(Speed 2016), human lives, particularly those of the most oppressed, are rendered irrelevant. Guatemala, Honduras, and Mexico are characterized today by an extraordinary level of violence and impunity that are products of this social dynamic. It is a dynamic that the United States also participates in, both as a primary market for illegal goods ranging from drugs to trafficked persons and through U.S.-based actors that form the northern flank of the networks of traffickers moving the goods.

It is now well documented that neoliberalism has increased social inequality (J. L. Collins, Di Leonardo, and Williams 2008; Ostry, Loungani, and Furceri 2016; Wade 2004). In Latin America, this has had a disproportionate effect on Indigenous people, already the most economically marginalized, which in turn has had, among other outcomes, an influence on increased migration (Aquino Moreschi 2009; Fox and Rivera-Salgado 2004b). Perhaps not surprisingly, given the unleashed illegal economies managed by shadowy and sometimes not-so-shadowy networks, complex networks have also developed to exploit the vulnerability of migrants. As Casillas has documented regarding Central American migrants moving through Mexico, "[There] evolved a number of sophisticated organizations dedicated, along the lines of division of labor, to different kinds of tasks—recruitment, relocation, patrol, monitoring, collusion with public officials, security, collection of funds, and kidnapping of immigrants, as well as the temporary use of immigrants for movement of drugs. . . . Gangs of robbers specializing in attacking and stealing from undocumented immigrants have appeared along the routes followed by these immigrants. They profit from the immigrants, either on their own or in conspiracies with criminal gangs and/or public safety officers" (2011:300). Thus, multilayered dangers faced by Indigenous women migrants are perpetrated by individuals, loosely coordinated groups, and highly organized networks of people, including public officials.

Marleny[2] was born in northern Honduras. Her mother abandoned the family when she was small, and Marleny was raised for several years by her father and callous stepmother. She would pray for her mother to return, sure that she would bring the love and protection she needed. When she was six, her mother did return. She had remarried and wanted to claim the children. Marleny was overjoyed, thinking that now her life was going to be happy. That dream was short-lived. Her stepfather treated her and her siblings harshly, and they had to work hard despite their young age. Within a year, her stepfather began sexually abusing her, though she was only seven years old. She did not tell her mother because she believed her mother loved her new husband more than she loved Marleny and would choose him over her. The abuse continued for five years, until Marleny was old enough to finally say "ya no" (no more) to her stepfather. But by that time her brother had begun being abusive, beating her. Finally, seeing few options to avoid the violence of her existence, she fled home at the age of fourteen.

Marleny had a little money saved, which she used to make her way to the Mexican border. She traveled from Honduras with a couple, and together they crossed into Tapachula, where they boarded the train that migrants refer to as La Bestia (The Beast). Shortly after the train left Tapachula, a group of Maras who had boarded with them ("como gente" [like people], Marleny said) pulled out guns and knives and began to wreak havoc among the travelers on the roof of the train, in what Marleny referred to as a calvario (siege). Men and women alike were robbed. Marleny watched in terror as women were raped and men strip-searched and anally assaulted with a pole. She witnessed the Maras rape one young woman, kill her, then toss her off the train. Marleny saw her body torn to pieces under the wheels of the train. Terrified and traumatized, she leapt from the roof of the moving train when it slowed as it approached the town of Arriaga, injuring her leg. Three Maras chased her but left her alone when she reached the town because there were people around. Frightened, injured, and thirsty, Marleny approached a house and asked for water.

The couple there took her in and told her they would help her. She trusted them and stayed with them for nearly two months. During that time, she encountered the couple with whom she had come from Honduras. However, they were hanging around with one of the Maras she had seen on the train, so she was distrustful of them. Then she learned that the older couple who had taken her in were attempting to sell her to work in a brothel. She fled their house, ending up in the company of the only other people she knew, the Honduran couple.

Together, they boarded another train, attempting to get farther north. However, the train was stopped by Mexican immigration officials (or police; Marleny wasn't sure) who ordered all the immigrants off. The commander of the group told Marleny that if she had sex with him, he would let the whole group go. Marleny, in a burst of anger, told him she would rather die than sleep with a pig. He punched her, with closed fist, in the face, knocking her to the ground. Another girl agreed to have sex with him in exchange for releasing the group. He had relations with her but refused to let the group go. When he threatened to kill Marleny, she told him she wasn't afraid, even though she was. He called her a "girl with a lot of balls" and expelled the group to Guatemala.

That was one of many deportations Marleny would experience as she tried to escape Tapachula, as many as thirty, she believes.

It was during this time that she got caught alone in a cemetery with the Mara her Honduran friends hung around with. He raped her on top of a crypt. Marleny closed her eyes and became, she said, "like a dead person." She never told anyone about that rape until the day she relayed it to me, almost as if it took her by surprise. "I had blocked it out completely," she said, voice wavering. Not long after, she, the Honduran couple, and the Mara who raped her were deported to Guatemala again. In a town near the border, the Mara was caught raping a woman. Townspeople, enraged, dragged him out and burned him alive. "I don't remember his face," Marleny said, "I don't remember what color his eyes were, but I remember his screams."

Marleny was also being used by the Honduran couple, who would force her to go out and panhandle and bring them the money. She had a jacket given to her by her father that she dearly loved, and they would hold her jacket to ensure that she would return. Finally, she built up her courage and decided to free herself, leaving the jacket behind. After fleeing, she found herself alone and hungry, and approached a woman sweeping outside her home, offering to exchange work for food. The woman took her in, and she began to work as a live-in housekeeper. Though the job did not pay much, it provided her meals and a roof over her head. It was while she was there that a young man began approaching, asking her to go out with him. Eventually she agreed, she said, because he was from a good family. On their first date, instead of taking her to a movie as he had promised, he took her to a hotel, where he forced himself on her. The rape left her pregnant, a fact she would not realize for five months. When the doctor informed her, he had to explain what "You are pregnant" meant and how it had come about. When her employer learned that she was pregnant, she fired her, tossing her into the street and calling her a puta *(whore). Marleny was terrified and had no idea what to do.*

Eventually, lacking any other options, she decided to approach the parents of the young man who had raped her and ask for support for the child. They agreed to this, but what at first seemed like a good thing would later turn dark, as two years later the grandparents used her illiteracy to trick her into signing papers ceding custody to them under the pretense of registering the child's birth. When she tried to fight this, they threatened to turn her in to Mexican immigration officials. The grandparents pressured her to go to the United States, telling her she would need to give them lots of money to get her son back. Seeing no other option, Marleny decided to depart for the United States,

*in the hope that there she could gather sufficient resources to satisfy them. She
left with "much pain in her heart" and a desperate desire to recover her son.*

*Marleny has been in the United States for fourteen years. Though she has
occasionally been able to talk to him by phone, she has not seen her son again.*

Perhaps what is most striking about Marleny's story are the multiple and
intersecting people seeking to exploit her. She is particularly vulnerable in
the liminal space of being undocumented—and a child—in southern
Mexico. Multiple actors and social dynamics come into play to create the vortex
of violence and risk Marleny was caught in. Wendy Vogt, who conducted
extensive fieldwork on the Central American migrant trail in southern
Mexico, has the following to say of the systematic exploitation migrants face:
"Each year, hundreds of thousands of people from Guatemala, El Salvador,
and Honduras attempt to cross Mexico, where they regularly encounter
abuse, rape, dismemberment, and death. While Central Americans have historically encountered abuse in Mexico . . . in recent years, direct violence
and exploitation have become far more systematic and inescapable"
(2013:764). We can see how Marleny was subject to this systematic and inescapable exploitation. She herself characterized it this way, saying, "It was
like a nightmare. Like I would never get out of there, never in my life. I could
not trust anyone." In order to unpack Marleny's story, I will explore the intersecting and interrelated dynamics one by one. In this chapter, I will look
at organized social violence in gangs and cartels, as well as the role of both
Mexican officials and the Mexican state in the violence. (Other aspects of
Marleny's story will be taken up in chapter 5.)

When Marleny first told me about her journey, the "siege" of the Maras
on the train floored me. Many women's stories are also marked by gang
activity—recall Estrella, who traveled with a group of young men from Guatemala City who were fleeing gang violence and threats and, on their trip,
encountered gang members from Maras on the train. Youth gangs (the two
most significant are the Mara Salvatrucha and the Eighteenth Street Gang)
are a significant aspect of the socially organized violence affecting people
throughout Mexico and much of Central America, and they are intimately
bound up with international traffickers, domestically based organized-
crime syndicates, and government agents, including police, military, and
immigration. Along with its lost promises of democracy and rights, neoliberalization brought increased levels of poverty, inequality, and unemployment. These conditions, as Elana Zilberg demonstrates in *Space of*

Detention, combined with the United States' deportation of gang members after the end of the Central American wars and its exportation of extreme policing strategies, creating conditions—what Zilberg terms "neoliberal securityscapes"—that have proved fertile ground for the growth of gangs in Central America (2011:3; see also Velasquez 2017; Vogt 2013). Even research by the U.S. Congressional Research Service acknowledged the role of U.S. deportations and policing in creating the problem: "The federal response to the MS-13 and M-18 gang problem has largely involved the enforcement of criminal and immigration laws, including the deportation of alien gang members. More recently, federal efforts have focused on prosecuting gang members under the Racketeer Influence and Corrupt Organizations (RICO) statute. Deported alien gang members have established MS-13 and M-18 gang cliques in their home countries, and some experts suggest that U.S. deportation policies have effectively transported U.S.-styled gang culture to parts of Central America and Mexico" (Franco 2007:1). The current street gangs in Mexico and Central America reproduce and perhaps even concentrate the patriarchal gender norms of the larger societies they are embedded in, exhibiting extreme and often violent notions of masculinities, as well as strong misogynistic tendencies (Olivera 2010:57). In her path-breaking fieldwork on masculinities among youth gangs in El Salvador, Elizabeth Velasquez (2017) demonstrates how these violent masculinities are tied to masculinist state making during the Salvadoran Civil War and in the post–peace accord era, and she shows how these ties are still present in the contemporary period. Undoubtedly, the same is true for Guatemala and Honduras. Further, the recent history of violence during the Central American wars of the 1980s set the frame for ongoing "violent pluralities" (Vogt 2013 citing Arias and Goldstein 2010) of state and nonstate actors. As I noted in the last chapter, for Guatemala, the violence of these wars was gendered, and that also sets a particular frame for the ongoing violence.

The gangs control the train routes and ride the trains, committing assaults, robberies, and rapes. People are so vulnerable to abuses on these trains that they are known collectively as "La Bestia" (The Beast) or *el tren de la muerte* (death train) (O. Martínez 2010; Nazario 2007). Dominguez Villegas (2014) describes the train: "As many as half a million Central American immigrants annually hop aboard freight trains. . . . The cargo trains, which run along multiple lines, carry products north for export. As there are no passenger railcars, migrants must ride atop the moving trains, facing physical dangers that range from amputation to death if they fall or are pushed. Beyond the dangers of the trains themselves, Central American migrants are subject to extortion and violence at the hands of the gangs and organized-crime groups that control the routes north." Marleny and Estrella were both confronted with precisely this kind of attack by Maras in their life-threatening experiences on the train north. In the words of Digna, who is introduced later in this chapter, "Crossing Mexico isn't easy. It's horrible; the entire way we are risking our lives. There are many bad people, charging 'taxes' [meaning robbing migrants]. They do this throughout Mexico, the whole way." As Dominguez Villegas's report indicates, the gangs control the routes, making them virtually unavoidable as one moves north, especially if it is on the trains.

Beyond committing offenses on the trains, gangs, working with cartels or local authorities and even the train conductors, often carry out kidnappings from the trains for ransom. Marleny experienced something like this when uniformed men stopped their train and robbed and sexually assaulted the migrant passengers. Police regularly work with rather than against the gangs. While some analysts interpret this as a form of "irregular warfare" against legitimate government institutions, in which the police, the judiciary, and entire local and departmental governments are plagued by criminal infiltrators (see Brands 2015 on Guatemala), other authors see it more as a "perversion" of the state itself than a simple corruption problem (Martinez 2014). In many areas, youth gangs are also closely linked with or formed by the cartels, serving almost as a paramilitary civilian enforcement wing.

Digna, a Garifuna woman from Honduras, was born in San Pedro Sula and grew up impoverished with her single mother and four siblings. As a young woman, she formed a relationship with a man whom she would spend the next nine years with, bearing three children, two girls and a boy. Her partner began using drugs and terrorized her for years with physical violence, breaking her nose and jaw and leaving her constantly bruised. He engaged in psychological abuse as well: during the day, he would force her and the children out of the house, and at night he would hurl verbal insults at her. He did not work and would take the money she earned selling meat to buy drugs. Then he began coming home drugged up on cocaine and marijuana and raping her. Several times she left him, going back to her mother's house, but he threatened to take her children, and she was particularly afraid he would rape the girls, so she would concede to his demands and return. Finally, in 2008 she decided to leave him and went to a women's shelter with her children.

By that time, he had joined a gang and was involved in stealing cars, selling drugs, and killing people, and she was terrified that the people he was involved with would hurt her and her children. Eventually, an opposing gang became vengeful after he killed someone from their gang. Despite the fact that she was no longer with him, members of the opposing gang began to threaten to rape and kill her and her children. They told her that if she wanted to keep her house in the Rivera Hernandez area of San Pedro (a very violent area), she would need to carry drugs for them in her vagina. She was forced to pay them one hundred lempira a day to keep her mother and children safe, a huge sum for a woman selling meat for a living. She knew the gang members—they were all locals, people she had gone to school with as a child. In 2013 she began dating a man named Marlon. He was a good partner and helped her make the payments to keep her house. However, Marlon was also being harassed and threatened by the gangs. Both his father and brother had been murdered, in 2010 and 2012, respectively, in the city of La Ceiba.

Finally, in November 2015, gang members came to the house and told her she had twenty-four hours to get out or they would kill her and her family. They fled, hiding in a nearby neighborhood, but the gang members found them. She and Marlon decided to flee. Leaving the children with her mother, they departed early the next morning by bus for Guatemala. When they reached El Naranjo on the Guatemalan border with Mexico, they called her mother. She said the gang members had already been there, looking for her. Digna and Marlon crossed a river to enter Mexico, then walked all day and night to reach Tenosique (about sixty miles from El Naranjo). There, they began "the terror of crossing Mexico." In Tierra Blanca, Veracruz, they caught La Bestia for the first time. On the journey, they were forced off the train by "the ones who charge taxes," criminal gangs that monitor the rails, robbing and raping immigrant riders. Digna had to jump off the train, injuring her hand in the process. Finally, they reached Nuevo Laredo, only to find that the polleros charged $1,500 to help them cross into the United States. They had no money at all by the time they reached the border, so they found work in a junkyard. A few weeks later, when they attempted to cross the river to Laredo, Texas, they were apprehended by the U.S. Border Patrol.

Digna experienced the intersection of domestic and gang violence, as the gendered and misogynistic aspects of gang life permeated their domestic environment. Again, gender violence presents a clear site for observing Das's "connect[ion of] the national to the domestic," as well as "deep connections between the spectacular and the everyday" (2008:283). What might otherwise be categorized as "domestic" or "generalized" violence in fact bears clear marks of the effects of much broader ideologies and social dynamics.

Honduras, known in recent years as the murder capital of the world, could also be called the impunity capital of the world. With a 2012 peak of more than seven thousand murders, in 2016 there were more than five thousand. A study by the Alliance for Peace and Justice, a Honduran NGO, showed that between 2010 and 2013, only 3.7 percent of homicides resulted in conviction; and in 2014, Honduras's conviction rate for murder was 1 percent (Gurney 2014). Within Honduras, the city of San Pedro Sula, where Digna lived, is arguably the most violent—indeed, it is often ranked as the single most violent city anywhere in the world, with a murder rate of 142 per 100,000 inhabitants (Pachico 2015; see also Seguridad, Justicia y Paz 2015). The city is divided into the rival street gang territories of the Mara Salvatrucha and the Eighteenth Street Gang. Descendants of gangs formed in Los Angeles and deported to Central America in the 1990s, their ranks were fed by economic disaster in Honduras and consolidated by the *mano dura* (iron fist) policies of the government in the late 1990s, and they were then emboldened by alliances with Mexican drug traffickers moving cocaine through the country.[3] According to InSight Crime's (2015) special report, the emergence of street gangs happened relatively quickly in Honduras:

> In the late 1990s, following legislation in the United States that led to increased deportation of ex-convicts, numerous MS13 and Barrio 18 members arrived in the country. By the early 2000s, these two gangs, along with several local groups, had begun a bloody battle for territory—and the extortion revenue and drug markets that goes with it—that continues to this day. The government responded by passing so-called "iron fist" legislation and arresting thousands of suspected gang members. Instead of slowing the growth of gangs, however, the policy allowed them to consolidate their leadership within the prison system, expand their economic portfolios and make contact with other criminal organizations.

All of these dynamics led to a rapid rise in gang activity, which would then combine with other dynamics, both domestic and international, to render gang activity one of the most serious problems Honduras is facing.

As the foregoing discussion indicates, the rise in organized crime in Honduras and Guatemala (as well as El Salvador) was not independent of dynamics with other countries, particularly the United States but also with Mexico. During the 1980s, Honduras served as the "hub of Ronald Reagan's counter-insurgency campaigns against guerrilla forces elsewhere in Central America" (Gordon and Webber 2013:17). The end of the guerrilla insurgencies in Guatemala and El Salvador and the Sandinista revolutionary government in Nicaragua set the stage, Gordon and Webber argue, "for the neoliberal pacification of Central America . . . over the course of the 1990s" (2013:17). Neoliberal restructuring was of course not limited to a Central American pacification process, as it was underway in Mexico starting with the structural adjustment policies of the 1980s, and in many other countries in Latin America as well. In Honduras, already the second-poorest country in the hemisphere, it resulted in "socioeconomic catastrophe" (Gordon and Webber 2013:17).

It was in this context that the government of Manuel Zelaya emerged in 2006, bringing with it a number of progressive policy positions, including support for the country's Indigenous rights movements in the struggle to resist extractive industries (Vacchio 2017). That same year, Mexican president Felipe Calderón launched a military crackdown on the drug trade (further discussed later in this chapter) and Central America's Northern Triangle — Guatemala, Honduras, and El Salvador — began experiencing increased drug-trafficking activity and much higher rates of violence. This process replicated the "balloon effect" previously experienced by Mexico after the implementation of Plan Colombia, which was conceived at the end of the 1990s.

Within a couple of years, Zelaya's policies had raised the hackles of the country's economic and military elites. That year, when Zelaya scheduled a public referendum on whether a constitutional assembly should be formed, the military seized power and named Congressional Speaker Roberto Micheletti president. Zelaya was put on a plane out of the country in his pajamas. U.S. officials, in particular then–Secretary of State Hillary Clinton, played a significant role in preventing Zelaya's return to office and the junta's consolidation of power in the face of massive nonviolent protests.[4] Despite the fact that the U.S. government's own ambassador requested that the United States refuse to recognize the illegal coup, and the Organization of American States, the Rio Group, and the UN General Assembly all called for the immediate and unconditional return of Zelaya, the United States did nothing. As Alexander Main explains, "Condemnations of the coup and the coup government of Roberto Micheletti came from every corner of the hemisphere, marking the gains made by progressive forces since the 1970s and 1980s, when military dictatorships were the prevailing form of regime throughout the region. Yet the Obama administration remained stuck in its default position as regional hegemon, adopting a position of complacency toward the coup government by failing to carry out any effective sanctions and by never clearly calling for Zelaya's reinstatement" (2010:16). Clinton would later acknowledge in her autobiography *Hard Choices* that she instead made plans with Mexico to keep Zelaya out and move toward elections. Those elections would turn out to be highly undemocratic, prompting the Organization of American States to draft a resolution that would have refused to recognize Honduran elections. However, the U.S. State Department blocked its adoption.[5]

The power vacuum produced by the coup and its aftermath, which included massive repression of protesters, opened the door for the expansion of illegal drug activity and the consolidation of power by cartel gangs and street gangs. As Tracy Wilkinson of the *Los Angeles Times* reports: "In the years since a 2009 military coup sent Honduras into a tailspin, unemployment and underemployment rates have doubled while the number of people living in extreme poverty has skyrocketed. . . . The mayhem is compounded by political killings, mostly of leftist activists and those demanding land rights in this throwback semi-feudal country, and vigilante slayings by some police units. It's made even worse by the inability or unwillingness of authorities to investigate crime in a nation where almost every family has had a relative killed, kidnapped or attacked."[6] Overarching illegality and impunity, combined with violent repression of opposition[7] and massive poverty, dovetailed with burgeoning drug trafficking displaced by the Mexican "drug war." The violence escalated accordingly, causing Honduras to become — for a time — the country with the highest murder rate in the world.

Not insignificantly, as Chris Loperena has shown, the coup-imposed government also quickly began implementing legislative measures that reconstituted Indigenous land as "emptied land" and approving bids for extractivist industries throughout the national territory. Loperena ties this directly to settler logics, concluding, "The extractivist development model that congealed in the wake of the coup against Zelaya is predicated on both the forcible removal *and* the elimination of Indigenous and black peoples. . . . These contemporary processes must be contextualized historically and understood as a legacy of the settler violence on which the contemporary state was constituted" (2017:806–7).

Like Honduras, Guatemala saw transnational organized crime and gang activity rise in the Calderón "drug war" period. Returning to Ysinia's story, for example, it reached a crisis when her threatening husband sent a relative who is an armed gang member to surveil and threaten her. That he had an armed gunman handy raises the specter of the complex and interrelated dynamics of the expansion of organized crime, increasing prevalence of armed gang members, and increased militarization. Armed men (Ysinia used the word *sicario*, which means "hit man") on the streets are most often a by-product of the ever-expanding tentacles of the drug cartels (Grayson 2010; McDonald and Hawkins 2013; Report to the UN High Commissioner for Human Rights Committee 2011). The conjunction of cartels with the police and the gangs that maintain cartel operations on the streets means that virtually everyone is controlled by their activity. Though her full story is not included in this book, Nadania's experience is illustrative of this point.[8] She fled her home in Honduras after she witnessed a murder on a bus carried out by local gangs linked to drug cartels, who she referred to simply as "the men who run the town." Two days after witnessing the murder, her small storefront was openly fired on. She fled, believing that the assassins from the bus had come to silence her. Leaving Honduras did not free her from danger, as she, like both Ysinia and Estrella, was held for ransom by cartel gangs in northern Mexico. Marleny also had multiple interactions with cartel gangs:

> *Marleny made her way north in the armored truck hired by a* narcotraffi-cante. *She met him through a friend, in a cafeteria in Tapachula. Her brother had just arrived from Honduras with the intention of making his way to the United States, where another of her brothers now lived. She herself had not yet made the decision to go, not wanting to leave her son behind. She was talking to her friend about how to help her brother make the journey she had tried so many times, when the man approached and offered to help her brother. "I like to help Central American immigrants," he said. At first she said no, but he insisted and offered to send him safely in a private truck and for free. Eventually, she agreed. Her brother was taken to Ciudad Victoria, and the* narcotrafficante *began to pressure Marleny. He became obsessed with her, pressuring her to sleep with him. One day she came home and found him in her house. She gave in to sleeping with him, afraid he would harm her son or her brother if she didn't do what he wanted. "Basically, he had me in his hands," she said. Seeing herself trapped, and increasingly certain that she would not get her son back (nor would it have been safe, under the circumstances), she convinced the* narcotrafficante *to send her to the United States to see her brother who lived in Texas, with the promise that she would return and marry him. She was taken to her brother in Ciudad Victoria, and together they were held in a hotel in Reynosa, waiting to cross*

the border to McAllen, Texas. Eventually, in a desperate move to escape the hotel, she and her brother turned themselves in to the U.S. Border Patrol and asked for asylum.

In border cities like Reynosa, popularly known as "the city where cartels rule," the cartels control many people on the street, including newspaper sellers, taxi drivers, and street kids, who report on the movements of police, soldiers, and also immigrants.[9] In the course of several years gathering women's migration stories, I met only one woman who came through Reynosa without being held for ransom. Rosa told me the story of how, after trying unsuccessfully to cross into the United States with a false ID, she was deported to Reynosa. She had been there less than an hour when she was detained by armed gunmen. "They knew the minute we entered the city," she said. One woman I spoke with was even deposited on the U.S. side of the border near McAllen after her ransom was paid by a relative in the United States, demonstrating the ways in which the work of the traffickers and the kidnappers was connected in larger networks. The vulnerability of Central American migrants to these cartels, which control everything and everyone in their territories, is tremendous. In 2010 the Mexican National Human Rights Commission reported that nearly ten thousand migrants had been abducted, mainly for ransom, over a period of just six months. Notably, nearly 50 percent of those interviewed said public officials had played a direct role in their kidnapping.[10]

Indeed, though the cartels have been said to constitute a virtual parallel power to the state in Mexico, and increasingly in Guatemala and Honduras (Fregoso and Bejarano 2010a; Report to the UN High Commissioner for Human Rights 2011), *parallel* is in fact the wrong word, as it suggests too many degrees of separation between the state and the cartels. That line of separation is actually quite porous, and the participation of many high-ranking government and military officials in narco-politics is well documented, as most spectacularly evidenced by the 2012 indictment of four high-ranking military generals, one of them the former undersecretary of defense, on charges of collaborating with drug traffickers (see Hernández 2012 for other cases).[11] In *Drug Lord*, Poppa writes, "The dark face of Mexico involved not just collusion with organized crime, but actually encouraging and regulating it. It was a system of command and control that ran through the country like the arteries and veins of a body, with its heart in Mexico City" (2010:xiv). Thus, while the violence perpetrated by cartels might seem to be a separate category from state violence, the state and its agents are active participants in the illegal economy and its violence. Nowhere was this evidenced more clearly than in the case of the forced disappearance of forty-three normal school students in Ayotzinapa, Guerrero. A 608-page report released in April 2016 by the international investigative body of the Organization of American States conclusively argues that the attacks on the students were coordinated by the C-4, the central command of state security forces, including municipal and federal police and the Mexican Army (Grupo Interdisciplinario de Expertos Independientes 2016).[12] The report details the students' abduction from a protest by police forces, who then turned them over to the cartel gang Guerreros Unidos on the orders of the local police chief, who was acting with the knowledge of, and possibly on the orders of, the mayor of the town. The report threw a blistering light on the terrible fact most people suspected or knew: that there is effectively no separation between the state and the cartels. Though the bodies of the students were never recovered, the search for them led to the discovery of half a dozen mass graves full of unidentified bodies.[13]

Other mass graves full of Central American bodies found along the migrant route shed a harsh light on the fact that the kidnappings of migrants do not always end in ransom and release. Notable was the mass grave discovered in April 2011 in San Fernando, Tamaulipas, about eighty miles south of the Texas border, containing fifty-nine bodies.[14] This was in the same area where seventy-two migrants, mostly from Central America, were found shot to death at a ranch the previous summer. Survivors reported that they had been attacked by cartel gang members after they refused to work for the cartel.[15] Police blamed the Zetas cartel for the killings. The mass killing of immigrants took a horrific turn in 2012, when the warring Zetas and Sinaloa cartels engaged in a practice of mass body dumping, apparently of people kidnapped randomly off the street, as a way to mark territory incursions and sow terror. In what Campbell refers to as "narco-propaganda," a "distinctive form of communication and discourse" used by the cartels, they sent messages to other cartels and to the public via grisly murders (2012:61). In April 2012, near the Texas border and the towns of Reynosa and McAllen, forty-nine bodies were dumped on a highway. They could not be readily identified because their hands, feet, and heads had been cut off. However, the fact that there had been no mass kidnapping reported and that this took place on a major migration route led authorities to believe many of the bodies were Central American migrants. One of the few bodies they were able to identify was that of Jose Yovanny Bocel, an Indigenous man from Guatemala.[16] Impunity for these mass killings is nearly total: in 2017 the United Nations Committee on the Protection of the Rights of All Migrant Workers and Members of Their Families (CMW) expressed deep concern at the "serious irregularities in the investigations carried out to identify the perpetrators and the victims of the massacres in the states of Tamaulipas and Nuevo León between 2010 and 2012, for which no one has yet to be punished" (CMW 2017:6).

Clearly, undocumented immigrants are, by definition, a vulnerable group that is subject not only to robbery and kidnapping, but even to mass murder as pawns in the power battles of cartels. However, Indigenous people stand out from other migrants and are correspondingly even more vulnerable. They stand out phenotypically and sometimes because of their dress and language ability. For women with limited Spanish, the entire experience of migration may be made more difficult by a limited understanding of what is happening and a lack of ability to communicate about it. This can greatly increase their vulnerability to violence, as we saw in Ysinia's story about the woman who was beaten by their captors. Social class also plays a role. Several non-Indigenous women migrants of middle-class professional backgrounds have told me that they stayed in their *polleros'* homes while waiting to cross the border, even eating with their families at the table. It is hard to imagine an Indigenous woman being hosted in this way, and while waiting on the streets they are at risk for kidnappings and assaults like those suffered by Ysinia, Estrella, and Rosa. Perhaps most importantly, Indigenous migrants are racialized through tropes that render them valueless and marked for death. Thus, it is not surprising that when abandoning her to likely death or arrest in the desert, Virgilia's *pollero* specifically referenced her Indigenousness through his racial epithet.

Like interpersonal violence, socially organized violence, as it affects Indigenous women migrants, is a product of histories of gendered state violence and the ongoing and pervasive racism and misogyny that continue to structure daily life and underpin privilege. Patriarchal structures live in both street gangs and cartels, reflecting and reproducing in extreme form the norms of society at large (Jiménez Váldez 2014; Váldez Cárdenas 2010). Further, all these forms of violence and impunity are given new ferocity when unleashed in the context of a neoliberalism taken to the extreme, where the only law that matters is the law of supply and demand, and the only logic that of the profit motive. Human lives, particularly those of the most oppressed, are rendered irrelevant.

The Blurry Line: The State and Illegality in Mexico

As we saw in relation to socially organized violence, the blurry lines between the Mexican government, its agents, and organized crime mean that the state is heavily implicated in the violence, even in spaces of "illegality" that purportedly function outside state control. However, it is not necessary to look to such "illegal" spaces to see gender, race, and class violence being perpetuated. These forms of violence are part of state ideology and discourse, as well as the practices of the agents of the state.

The first detention of Ysinia's journey was by Mexican immigration agents in the state of Chiapas, and in this context she encountered new forms of interpellation by the state she had entered. The "national security state" in Mexico at the time was defined by the ostensible war on drug trafficking. Upon taking office in Mexico in 2006, Felipe Calderón militarized antidrug efforts, waging a "war" against the cartels that became notorious as much for its brutality as for its ineffectiveness (Campbell 2009). It also undermined the rule of law and quickly dispensed with the observance of civil liberties. The military proceeded to commit numerous human rights abuses, including abductions, torture, rape, and extrajudicial killings. The number of human rights complaints against the military at the Mexican National Human Rights Commission dramatically increased, from 182 in 2006 to 1,230 in 2008, of which only 3 percent resulted in a sentence (Corrales 2012). Further, the line between the government and the drug cartels it is ostensibly fighting is so blurry as to be functionally nonexistent. Campbell argues that in Mexico, "organized crime and official government are so tightly interwoven yet secretive that they indeed form an 'underground empire'" (2009:7 quoting Mills 1986). The clear participation of both the police and the military in illegal activities and violence is evidenced by the dramatic increase in violence whenever they were deployed during the Calderón administration's "war on drugs," a dynamic that contributed to nearly sixty thousand deaths and led to the six years he spent in office being referred to as the *sexenio de la muerte* (six-year presidential administration of death) (Hernández 2012). Rosalva Aída Hernández and I (Hernández and Speed 2012) have argued elsewhere that the Mexican government, in a desperate effort to show some gains in the flailing "war on drugs," increasingly criminalized poor, Indigenous people, imprisoning them with exorbitant sentences for minor drug offenses. Calderón's 2008 Penal Reform (Reforma Constitucional en Materia de Justicia Penal y Seguridad Pública) marked the shift from a neoliberal multicultural approach to a conservative authoritarian one. Designed to strengthen rule of law in the context of the war on drugs, the reform, particularly Articles 16 and 18, created a "state of exception" for people accused of involvement with organized crime and limited their constitutional rights' guarantees against abuses like being detained without charges and being incarcerated in special facilities far away from their homes and families. Indigenous people accused of relatively minor drug offenses (often in these situations they have been forced through violence or poverty to carry drugs), are locked away for extended periods completely disproportionate to their "crimes." Hernández and I write, "[During Calderón's administration], indigenous people have been [interpellated] by the state either as poor peasants who must be integrated to mega-development projects, or as criminals who should be incarcerated, applying a special legal regime intended for organized crime" (Hernández and Speed 2012:17, translation mine). Thus these reforms, rather than strengthening the rule of law, increased imprisonment rates and fortified the carceral state.

The "war on drugs" also led to increased patrolling of the southern border. In the early 2000s, the Fox administration, under pressure from the United States to stop the flow of drugs, broadened border patrol activities, increasing the danger for migrants in a region where they are as likely to meet violence and abuse from agents of the state as from criminals. Then, the discovery of mass graves filled with Central American migrants highlighted exactly how out of control the country was and significantly embarrassed the Calderón administration, which responded by upping immigration patrols again. Their detention of Ysinia was enmeshed in these dynamics — the immigration agent's racialized, gendered, and even class-tinged remarks about the "Indita" were but the latest iteration of subjugation, pointing as they did to the implied "danger" of winding up in a mass grave and suggesting that if she did, it would be her own fault for having had the audacity as an Indigenous women to venture to leave home. As previously noted, while in Mexico race has historically played a role in defining Indigenous-state relations that is different from the role it plays in Guatemala because of the hegemony of the discourse of *mestizaje*, racism against Indigenous people remains high nonetheless. And in the neoliberal moment, even as the state pursued limited reforms that would move it toward multiculturalism and increased rights, the Zapatista uprising and national Indigenous organizing disrupted the narrative, and the state responded by interpreting Indigenous people as potential subversives and terrorist threats, a fact that is particularly palpable in the state of Chiapas, where Ysinia was apprehended. In making these comments, the immigration officials were mobilizing long-standing discourses of race and gender that hold sway both in Indigenous communities and outside them: Indigenous women who leave the community bring danger on themselves and thus are to blame for rape or other violence when it happens to them.

As both Ysinia's and Estrella's stories reflect, those dangers are real. Many women migrants are sexually assaulted or raped while crossing Mexico or crossing into the United States. A 2010 report by Amnesty International estimates that six out of ten migrant women and girls have experienced sexual violence at the hands of criminals, other migrants, or corrupt public officials. In 2017 the CMW expressed its concern about the continued "extremely serious impact of enforced disappearance on migrants and Mexican nationals in transit and the high levels of gender-based violence, particularly on the southern border" (CMW 2017:6). Notably, the committee also expressed that it was "very concerned at the allegations of involvement by public authorities, particularly the federal, state and municipal police, the widespread impunity frequently associated with such crimes and the low numbers of complaints" (CMW 2017:6). When Ysinia made it through her harrowing boat trip across the river, she was subject to gender violence by the men who brought her across and was nearly raped. Estrella was less fortunate, and while making her way north was assaulted by someone she believed to be a Mexican immigration official. Neither made a complaint.

State violence against Indigenous women is by no means limited to war or genocide. Agents of the state at all levels both act from and redeploy ideologies of race, class, and gender in their acts of violence against Indigenous women migrants, and they do so comfortably in the context of ideologically generated impunity. As Casillas puts it, "All these criminal practices, as well as the agents who commit them, go unpunished, [while] sexual abuse and rape leave their victims with indelible scars, not only from abortions, sexually transmitted diseases, and unwanted children, but also from the emotional aftermath and memories" (2011:301). Agents of the Mexican state engage directly in gender violence, but the state, in a more abstract sense, also facilitates it by failing to hold anyone accountable for it. The harms created extend well beyond the actual acts to the prolonged pain of injustice.

The violence and lack of accountability only increased under the administration of Enrique Peña Nieto (which was heavily implicated in the unresolved crimes in Ayotzinapa). Statistics released by the Mexican government in July 2017 showed that 12,155 homicide cases were opened between January and June, making it the deadliest first half of a year since the government began releasing crime data in 1997. Astonishingly, prosecutors opened 2,234 homicide investigations in the month of June alone, which was a 40 percent increase over June 2016 and an 80 percent increase over June 2015.[17] The previous month was even higher, with 2,452 cases opened, which meant that one person was murdered every twenty minutes in the month of May.[18] According to an International Institute for Strategic Studies survey on armed conflicts released in May 2017, Mexico was at that time the second-deadliest place in the world after Syria, with 22,967 homicides in 2016.[19] Tellingly, *Newsweek* also reported that the Mexican government disputed the institute's claim by noting that not all of the murder victims were killed in the drug war — some, they said, were victims of domestic violence. Revisiting my argument from chapter 2, I understand these forms of violence as heavily interrelated and also tightly bound to the state and its lack of accountability. The state's attempt to distance itself from some of the violence by designating it as domestic is unconvincing. The same *Newsweek* article cited Mexican security analyst Alejandro Hope, who suggested that the "structural problem" of impunity is responsible for all the violence, and, as we saw in chapter 2, that includes gender violence and feminicide.

However, while impunity is an important part of the state's role in the violence, there are larger structural aspects within which this impunity operates. One, I have argued, is neoliberal capitalism and its unleashed market logics, which gave rise to the neoliberal market society — a multicriminal one — in which all players are part of the illegality and no one is subject to the law. As an example specifically related to the most recent rise in violence in Mexico, one has to consider the industry-implicated epidemic of opioid addiction in the United States and the consequent increased demand.[20] The U.S. Drug Enforcement Agency (2016) reports that the vast majority of heroin in U.S. markets comes from Mexico and this increased cash flow has allowed cartels to fund stepped-up warfare. In addition, the United States' exportation of its "drug war" policies have been spectacularly unsuccessful, including targeting high-ranking cartel leaders such as Joaquín "El Chapo" Guzmán, who was extradited to the United States in 2018, leaving power vacuums that fuel power struggles between successors and further escalate the violence.[21] Thus, in neoliberal multicriminalism, both market forces and the networks of illegality that accompany them shape the lives of everyone, including Indigenous women migrants, and render them vulnerable to violence.

Further, as we shall see in greater detail in the next chapter, the U.S. state bears direct responsibility for the hardships endured as a result of its purposefully brutalizing immigration policies. In *The Land of Open Graves*, De

Leon writes, "The terrible things that this mass of migrating people experience en route are neither random nor senseless, but rather part of a strategic federal plan that has rarely been publicly illuminated and exposed for what it is: a killing machine" (2015:3). While De Leon is specifically referring to the "prevention through deterrence" policy that causes people to suffer and die in the Sonoran Desert, its applicability might be expanded to encompass more than the desert. Making the journey (and, as we shall see, entrance to the United States) harsh—for many, unsurvivable—allows the United States to "simultaneously use and hide behind the viciousness" of the journey and the engagement with the immigration system itself to deter others from coming (De Leon, 2015:3).

Within that context, settler-generated ideologies of race and gender work to create specific forms of vulnerability for Indigenous women, as we have seen in the stories of Ysinia, Marleny, Virgilia, Estrella, Euphemia, and Digna, rendering violence against them both legible and tolerable to the larger society. The Mexican immigration agent's comments to Ysinia make this clear: an Indigenous woman who leaves her assigned space and role is subject to potential gender violence, and this is expected and acceptable. Settler logics of race and gender continue to operate in the current neoliberal multicriminal moment in ways that are remarkably similar to their historical methods of operation, rendering Indigenous women vulnerable in different yet all too familiar ways.

I ARGUED IN chapter 2 that while state violence might seem quite distinct from interpersonal violence, both forms of violence are in fact intimately intertwined, mutually generative, and a product of settler-generated ideologies of gender, race, and class. The same is true for socially organized violence such as cartel or gang violence, which on its face might seem distinct from state violence. As we have seen in the stories in this chapter, the state is intimately involved in this socially organized violence, both as a direct perpetrator and through its utter failure to fulfill its duty of holding perpetrators accountable to the law. They are in fact all offspring of the same ideologies of power and oppression; they appear to be so closely interrelated that they are analytically inseparable. Thus, settler-generated ideologies, along with the specific histories of their deployments, again serve both to justify and to generate violence against Indigenous women in the context of their journeys north. These ideologies intersect with neoliberal logics of unbridled market forces to generate a context in which lawlessness and lack of accountability are the norm and not the exception. As neoliberal states abandon their populations to market forces, thrusting Indigenous people into ever-increasing levels of poverty and marginalization, those same market forces redefine the state itself. Violence and lack of accountability are not simply matters of criminal elements and corruption but rather are structural features of the neoliberal multicriminal settler state. As the women's stories in this chapter reflect, this generates a structural context in which Indigenous women migrants are multiply *vulneradas*—rendered vulnerable to violence again and again.

In the next chapter, I turn to the next phase of many women's experience: immigration detention in the United States and the multiple forms of violence that it entails. This provides an opening for a discussion of the United States not just as a participant in the massive markets and webs of illegal activity entailed by neoliberal multicriminalism but also as a state that generates (raced, gendered) violence through state interpellations and state subject-making in laws, policies, and actions.

CHAPTER FOUR

Carceral Containments

Captivity in the Homeland Security State

Apprehended at the U.S. border, Digna was separated from her partner, Marlon, and taken to the hieleras *(iceboxes), where she was put in a very cold room and given a Mylar blanket.*[1] *She spent two days sleeping on the floor with dozens of others packed in the room. When she was brought before an immigration judge, she admitted to crossing the border illegally but said that she had done it because her life was in danger. She was moved through a couple of detention facilities in Laredo over the next week, then transferred to the Hutto facility in Taylor. Terrified of being imprisoned and suffering from severe depression and anxiety, her health plummeted. As a Garifuna, she is an Indigenous Afro-descendant, and she suffers from sickle cell anemia. She also had severe gastritis, a product of her stress and trauma in Honduras. She advised the Corrections Corporation of America (CCA) repeatedly of her illnesses but received little treatment. Her blood pressure soared. She had nosebleeds and vomited blood. Her menstrual period ceased. Her feet swelled. She was twice infected with h-pylori bacteria from the food she was given in the detention center and also contracted scabies there. She was diagnosed with a herniated belly button and cysts on her breast and ovaries. Despite being given many pills, and injected with morphine on one occasion without her knowledge or approval, she got little relief from her escalating pain and suffering.*

In May, Marlon was deported to Honduras. In October, he was murdered.

When Digna participated along with many other women in the hunger strikes protesting the terrible food and health conditions and extended deten-tion periods, she was the first woman punished—first placed in isolation, then moved to a facility in Laredo, where activists who had visited her in Hutto and her pro bono attorney had difficulty reaching her. It was just after her move that she learned of Marlon's murder. Digna spent three more months in detention in Laredo. When she reported feeling ill there, she was taken to a medical isolation unit where they had previously held women with tuberculo-sis. Digna was infected.

Finally, Digna was released, after spending more than eleven months in detention. Her release was likely due to the public nature of the hunger strike and the fact that activists on the outside were actively campaigning for her release based on the gravity of her state of health. At the time of this writing, she awaits her immigration hearing, scheduled for 2019. She is without medical or psychological care and lives in constant fear for her children, now twelve, eleven, and nine, whom she left behind in Honduras.

Digna, fleeing gang violence in Honduras, was detained by the Border Patrol crossing the river into the United States. Ysinia, while escaping a sexual assault, was detained by the U.S. Border Patrol. Estella turned herself in, believing she had reached safety. Virgilia was apprehended after her *pollero* abandoned her in the desert. All were cast into the vast immigration detention system, where they remained for months. One common characteristic of nearly all the women whose stories I gathered was that they had been incarcerated for some period of time in the United States. The carceral nature of the U.S. national security state inevitably rendered its violence on them.

As Digna's devastating story reflects, like those of the women in previous chapters, the hardships experienced by Indigenous women migrants in their engagements with the U.S. immigration system are complex and often life-shattering. This is true for all immigrants, without a doubt, and in this chapter I examine how the state interpellates migrants through its laws and policies in the United States, and the ways these interpellations do violence to people's physical and emotional well-being. In particular, I will consider how Indigenous women migrants experience the state through immigration policing, detention, and deportation differently from other migrants because of their race and gender. As in the last two chapters, I will focus on the multiple ways that these women are *vulneradas* by "human caging" (Lytle Hernández 2017) in what Alfonso Gonzales has termed the "neoliberal homeland security state" (2013) and the particular role of settler-generated ideologies of race and gender that work to render them vulnerable in that context.

The Carceral Space of the Neoliberal Homeland Security State

The United States became the U.S. "homeland security state" (Gonzales 2013) in the post–9/11 period, with serious implications for immigrants. The U.S. immigration detention system has expanded dramatically, an expansion that began in the late 1990s but escalated after 9/11. As Casillas explains, "Following the events of September 11, the United States increased its measures for immigration and border control. Among the principal measures adopted were: the Patriot Act, 2001, which tripled the number of immigration inspectors, customs officials, and border patrol officers along the

Mexican border, increased the budgetary allowance for technological equipment, and reinforced regulations to block the entry of possible terrorists" (2011:299).[2] In 2003 the Immigration and Naturalization Service was dissolved and its functions were brought under the newly created Department of Homeland Security (DHS), the mission of which is defined in the Homeland Security Act (2002) as "preventing terrorist acts in the United States [and] reducing the vulnerability of the United States to terrorism." This move signaled an important shift—all immigrants, including refugees and asylum seekers, would be regarded as potential terrorist threats. In 2004 Congress linked that interpretation to incarceration, authorizing funds for the construction of up to forty thousand additional immigration detention bed spaces over the next five years through the Intelligence Reform and Terrorism Prevention Act. The following year, DHS implemented its Secure Border Initiative, which has as its stated goal "improving public safety by working to better identify, detain and ultimately remove dangerous criminal aliens from your community" (Immigration and Customs Enforcement [ICE] 2012). Thus, in the several years following the September 11, 2001 attacks, immigrants, including asylum seekers in civil proceedings, were recast at terrorists and criminals. As Martin (2011) notes, these criminalized migrant-subjects were rendered ineligible for the due process on which liberal legal regimes are based.

In the decade from 2001 to 2011, the yearly detention of noncitizens more than doubled, ballooning from 188,542 in 2001 (Office of the Federal Detention Trustee 2002) to 429,247 in 2011 (Simanski and Sapp 2012). This trend continued, and a report by the nonpartisan Migration Policy Institute (Meissner et al. 2013) showed that the Obama administration spent nearly $18 billion on immigration enforcement in 2012, significantly more than it spent on all the other major federal law enforcement agencies combined,[3] and detained a record 477,523 that year (Simanski 2014). While detentions dropped slightly in 2014 to 425,478, they have remained at more than double pre-2001 numbers.

In the 2000s the accelerated growth of the detainee population quickly began to tax existing facilities and detention centers. In a process closely linked to the rise of the for-profit prison industry, the U.S. government increased its contracts with the CCA and the GEO Group, private, publicly traded corporations, in order to accommodate its expanding immigration detention population (Feltz and Baksh 2009). A 2015 report showed that private prison corporations operated 62 percent of ICE immigrant detention beds that year, while nine of the ten largest ICE immigrant detention facilities are operated by for-profit prison corporations (Carson and Diaz 2015). Now operating a forty-thousand-bed system (more than 70 percent privatized), ICE manages the fastest-growing incarcerated population in the United States. While the size and scope of the United States' immigration detention population is unprecedented and shocking, it is perhaps unsurprising, considering that the country incarcerates nearly 2.5 million people—the world's largest prison population, both per capita and by sheer numbers of people locked up. ICE is unique among law enforcement agencies, however, in that it is subject to a mandatory bed quota based on language in the congressional appropriations law that requires it to maintain thirty-four thousand immigration detention beds that must be filled on a daily basis (a number that has steadily increased since its establishment in 2009),[4] ensuring profits for the private prison corporations.[5]

Thus, the massive expansion of immigration detention in recent years is intimately linked with the rise of the for-profit prison industrial complex, one of neoliberalism's more pernicious manifestations in the United States (see Alexander 2012; Gilmore 2007). The ideologies of the homeland security state interpellate immigrants as potential terrorists and dangerous criminals and generate masses of locked-up immigrants (including asylum seekers in civil proceedings who have committed no crime), producing the added effect of garnering massive profits for private prison corporations (Ackerman and Furman 2013). This shift to interpreting immigrants as terrorists and criminals thus intersected with the neoliberal state imperative of privatization, lack of regulation, and profit motive, making immigrants the fodder of the carceral state.

In *City of Inmates*, Kelly Lytle Hernández argues that "mass incarceration is mass elimination" (2017:1). Tying the "rise of human caging" directly to processes of settler elimination, she argues that mass incarceration is a mechanism of the settler drive to eliminate: "In addition to native elimination, settler societies strive to block, erase, or remove racialized outsiders from their claimed territory. Even as many settler societies depend on racialized workforces, settler cultures, institutions, and politics simultaneously trend toward excluding racialized workers from full inclusion in the body politic, corralling their participation in community life, and, largely shaped by rising and falling labor demands, deporting, hiding, or criminalizing them or otherwise revoking the right of racialized outsiders to be within the invaded territory" (2017:7–8). Lytle Hernández ably demonstrates how human caging as a settler eliminatory logic took different forms over time in the city of Los Angeles, in response to the changing labor needs of capital. Here, I argue that the human caging of immigrants is part of this settler drive to "revok[e] the right of racialized outsiders to be within the invaded territory" and took its particular subcontracted form in response to the neoliberal mandate for privatization.

T. Don Hutto and the "Kinder, Friendlier Detention" of the Obama Administration

> *Virgilia entered the Hutto visitation room looking pale and strained. We hugged, and tears came to her eyes as she sat down. "Any news?" I asked, knowing already the answer by her countenance. Her face crumpled and she muffled a small sob, with a sideways glance at the guard. "Nothing," she said. Virgilia was awaiting news of a date for her credible fear interview,[6] a crucial step that would put her into asylum proceedings and potentially—if she passed—allow her to get a bond out of detention. If she did not pass, she would be deported. Credible fear interviews usually happened fairly quickly—Virgilia's was inexplicably taking longer. She grew tenser by the day, worrying nonstop about the outcome and imagining all sorts of reasons for the delay. This day she said, "I think maybe they are not going to give me an interview. They will just send me back." I tried to explain that they have to give her an interview; they are required to do so by law. She looked unconvinced. I tried again, "They can't just send you back." Virgilia's face crumpled again, and through her tears she said, remarkably clearly, "But what if they do? Or what if my case is lost and they leave me here forever?"*

The T. Don Hutto facility, where Digna, Virgilia, Ysinia, Euphemia, and Estrella were detained, is a microcosm of these larger dynamics of the carceral homeland security state (figure 1). The CCA built the medium-security prison facility in 1995 as an income generator for the town of Taylor and Williamson County. It was reincarnated in 2006 as a "residential facility" for the detention of immigrant families. Secured by chain-link fences and patrol cars and situated between an empty field and a highway overpass, separated from the town by train tracks, the facility is difficult to access and largely invisible to the town's residents. Conditions at the prison during its period as a family detention center included compelling children to wear prison uniforms, keeping families in their cells twelve hours a day, guards threatening children with separation from their parents, and failing to provide adequate nutrition and medical care (Women's Commission for Refugee Women and Children and Lutheran Immigration and Refugee Service 2007). It quickly became

FIGURE 1 The T. Don Hutto Residential Center, run by the private prison corporation Corrections Corporation of America (now CivicCore). AP Photo/ Donna McWilliam, File.

an infamous symbol of expanded immigration policing, detention, and deportation.

In 2007 the American Civil Liberties Union (ACLU) and the University of Texas Law School, following on the advocacy of a coalition of immigrant rights and faith-based activists called Texans United for Families, sued ICE and DHS on behalf of twenty-six immigrant children detained with their parents at the T. Don Hutto detention center.[7] The lawsuit contended that the conditions inside the detention center violated numerous provisions of *Flores v. Meese*, a 1997 court settlement that had established minimum standards and conditions for the housing and release of all minors in federal immigration custody. Based on the understanding that holding children in the same conditions as adults are held was inhumane, the *Flores v. Meese* settlement agreement mandated that juveniles be afforded appropriate care and protection given their age and vulnerability, including that they not be housed in adult detention facilities, but rather in "safe and sanitary" facilities, and that they be provided fair opportunity for release on bond by taking affirmative steps to release them to appropriate family custody.[8]

Following the lawsuit and landmark settlement, and facing continuing protests over the practice, the Obama administration virtually ended family detention, announcing that families would no longer be detained at Hutto, no new family detention centers would be opened, and only one family detention center would remain open, located in Berks County, Pennsylvania, which had fewer than one hundred beds.[9] The children were released from the Hutto facility, which now houses only women.[10] Whether it acted in recognition of the moral sinkhole of immigration detention or in an effort to ward off future lawsuits, the administration undertook various efforts to create a "kinder, friendlier" detention experience for "low-risk" populations (principally asylum seekers). The Hutto facility was to serve as a model for this, and it was spruced up a bit, with one row of fencing and razor wire taken down outside and the cellblocks painted bright pink (figure 2).

However, though the settlement represented a victory both in forcing recognition that family detention violated the rights of minors and in securing their freedom during their legal processes, conditions for the women detained in Hutto following the lawsuit remained ripe for human rights violations. The women held in Hutto are isolated from their friends and families and still vulnerable to intimidation and abuse. The Hutto facility has been the subject of two federal sexual abuse investigations, and in 2011 a former guard, Donald Dunn, pleaded guilty to federal charges for sexually assaulting detained women.[11] All of the nine women assaulted by Dunn had been victims of previous gender violence and the assaults served to further traumatize them. The assaults occurred when Dunn was transporting women alone from the Hutto facility to the airport or bus station in nearby Austin. Documents obtained by the ACLU of Texas, which filed a lawsuit on behalf of the assaulted women in 2015, indicate that in addition to the seven known occasions on which Dunn assaulted a total of nine women, at least twenty male guards transported at least forty-four female

FIGURE 2 After a successful lawsuit against the Department of Homeland Security, Immigration and Customs Enforcement spiffed-up the detention center, even painting the cellblocks pink. AP Photo/Donna McWilliam, File.

detainees alone between December 2008 and May 2010, making it possible that many more assaults occurred and went unreported. The lawsuit alleges that ICE, Williamson County, and CCA were deliberately indifferent and willfully blind to the fact that Dunn and other employees regularly violated the rule that detainees not be transported without another escort officer of the same gender present. It characterizes the problems as "systemic," rather than a product of individual misbehavior or corruption.[12]

Yet ICE continued to tout the spruced-up facility as a "model" and went to work constructing a new facility in Karnes City, Texas, about an hour outside San Antonio, as a "low-risk" facility built on the model of Hutto. Bright blue paint (apparently a nod to the fact that this was originally intended to be a men's facility), flat-screen TVs in the rooms, a soccer field, and picnic tables on a bright green lawn characterized the new and improved Karnes. Like Hutto, it would be referred to as a "residential facility," and, we were told, those who would be held here would no longer be called "detainees," but rather "residents." Guards would be called "resident advisers." Taking reporters and advocates on a tour of the facility before it opened, the eager-to-impress ICE officials leading our tour asked our group with apparent sincerity, "We would like to have your suggestions: What else could we do to make it more comfortable?" An immigrant advocate, not convinced by the bright paint and shiny sports equipment, piped up, "How about a really big door marked EXIT?" The ICE officials were not amused, but the advocate had made his point. It was still a prison. A short time later, Karnes would be reassigned to house women and children when family detention, practically ended by the Obama administration, was reinitiated by the same administration in 2015 in response to the ostensible "crisis" of arriving refugee children and families fleeing the violence in Central America and, to a lesser extent, Mexico. Hilaria and her six-year-old son Elan were among them.

> In 2014 Hilaria left her home in San Marcos, Guatemala, with her young son, fleeing domestic violence. She entered the United States in Texas, part of a wave of refugee families that flowed into the country, striking terror in the heart of a xenophobic country already predicated on racialized understandings of good and bad immigrants. Like many others, they were cast into Karnes, one of the prisonlike facilities designated to incarcerate the women and children, and there they remained for eleven months. Though she passed her credible fear interview, Hilaria's asylum claim was eventually denied because of errors committed by her first attorney, but a new case was opened by her second pro bono lawyer on behalf of her son. Hilaria joined in the hunger strikes organized by women in the facilities to protest deplorable conditions, including lack of health care, sexual harassment, and unconscionably long incarceration. The private prison corporation GEO first retaliated by isolating women and moving many to distant locations, but eventually ICE conducted a mass release. Hilaria and Elan moved into Casa Esperanza, an immigrant shelter for families in Austin, Texas. She struggled to manage the huge monitoring chain shackled to her small ankle and sought work to sustain herself as she nervously awaited the outcome of Elan's case.

Karnes, Family Detention, and the Violence of Prolonged Incarceration

Hilaria and Elan were among the early arrivals at Karnes in 2015, when it was opened to receive families. Just five years earlier, the Obama administration had all but ended family detention after public pressure about the shameful practice of incarcerating children. Nevertheless, the administration renewed the practice of mass detention of immigrant families in 2014, after tens of thousands of families fleeing the violence in Central America and Mexico began arriving at the border. In July of that year, a family detention center was opened in Artesia, New Mexico, and shortly thereafter the administration announced that it would start detaining families at the 500-plus bed Karnes facility and expand the Berks County detention center. In its supplemental appropriations request to Congress that year, the administration asked for funding for up to 6,300 family detention beds across the country. There were a total of 3,700 beds in place by year's end, up from fewer than 100 at the beginning of the year (Grassroots Leadership 2016). Women and children refugees, already traumatized by the violence that forced them to leave home and violence experienced on their journeys north, were shunted into the new family prisons under conditions not at all unlike those that had previously been in place in Hutto.

As early arrivals at the Karnes facility, Hilaria and Elan watched as the facility filled up with women and children. Karnes is located in Karnes City, an oil-field town surrounded by ranches and pastures at the heart of the state's shale-fracking boom. As big-rig trucks full of fracked oil sped by at breakneck speeds on the highway outside, the refugee families inside were subjected to inedible food, inadequate medical care, and twice-daily body count regimes that dragged them out of bed before dawn. Accusations of abuses mounted, and in October 2014 attorneys from the Mexican American Legal Defense and Education Fund and the University of Texas School of Law filed a complaint to DHS. The complaint alleged "substantial, ongoing sexual abuse" at Karnes, including that staff had removed mothers from their cells at night, promising to help with their immigration cases in exchange for sexual favors, and groped women in front of children.[13]

Perhaps unsurprisingly, DHS, in its investigation of the allegations, found no wrongdoing.[14] The report from the inspector general offers as evidence of its findings that the guards and women alleged to have been involved in the sexual acts denied that they had done so, and the supervisors denied any knowledge of such acts. Additionally, the surveillance videotape they reviewed did not show evidence of such acts.[15] Apparently, this was enough to prove that no wrongdoing occurred in the eyes of DHS. The likelihood that the self-interested guards and supervisors, not to mention the terrified and vulnerable women detainees, might not have been entirely forthcoming about events was apparently not considered, nor was the possibility that guards might have been smart enough to circumvent surveillance cameras. Indeed, the Inspector General's Office seems to have been primarily concerned with the final point in its report that "ICE complied with the Prison Rape Elimination Act reporting requirements."[16]

Regardless of whether these egregious acts of power-wielding took place, numerous other serious abuses were occurring and were reported by women detainees and others who worked in the facility. For example, social worker Olivia López, who was employed in the Karnes facility in late 2014, testified before a congressional forum on family detention hosted by the Congressional Progressive Caucus and Democrats from the House Judiciary Committee in July 2015 that she had quit after being repeatedly instructed to engage in unethical practices.[17] She expressed her concern that "detainees' medical and psychological problems were being downplayed or ignored."[18] López gave specific examples. She was instructed to omit information about medical complaints in the files, including in one case of a woman having recurring headaches who had a history of brain aneurysms. In another case, López said, she noticed that a five-year-old girl, who had been raped and physically abused during the trip north, had lost weight and begun wearing diapers. When she reported this to her supervisor, a psychologist, he discharged the girl and noted in her file that she was sleeping and eating better. When López contested this by submitting another note reiterating that the girl had lost weight, a different supervisor rebuffed her, stating that she was mistaken.[19] Further, López substantiated the claims of women—Hilaria included—that they were retaliated against for participating in the hunger strike to protest abuses by being placed in isolation in the medical unit with their children, noting that her supervisor made an announcement that the warden wanted the "ringleaders" put in isolation.

The hunger strike in Karnes, in which as many as eighty women participated, was both an act of desperation and a critically important act of resistance. Begun in April 2015, it provided a vehicle for the women to draw attention to their prolonged detention, the terrible conditions they faced in the facility, and the injustice of detaining refugee families. A few months later, women in Hutto followed suit, and Digna was one of the strike initiators, along with twenty-six others, in October 2015. She was subject, as we saw, to precisely the kind of retaliation that López substantiated regarding the women in Karnes (figure 3).

Clearly, the kinder, friendlier model for immigrant incarceration proposed by the Obama administration was something less than kind and

Soy Hondureño

por medio de esta Carta estamos pidiendo que por
favor nos apoyen a salir de este lugar.

Me siento muy preocupada porque yo traendo mis pruebas
mean negado mi caso no se porque a nosotras de Segunda
no nos toman en cuenta si tenemos los mismos derechos
que todas.
y me querían aser firmar a la fuerza y me dijo el oficial
que si no firmo que me iba a meter a la cárcel
y medio la hoja de deportación y los de aslo me la hicieron
y yo tengo miedo regresar a mi pais porque tengo amenazas
de muerte en mi pais.
y por favor nesecitamos que ustedes nos apoyen.
Gracias

FIGURE 3   Digna's letter to the world explaining her participation in the hunger strike. The letter reads, "I am Honduran. With this letter we are asking that you please support us and help us get out of this place. I feel very worried because although I brought proof they have denied my case. I do not know why. They do not pay attention to us, even though we have the same rights as everyone else. And they wanted to force me to sign [probably a voluntary departure] and the official told me if I didn't sign that they were going to put me in jail and he gave me the paper for deportation and the ones for asylum and they detained me. I am afraid to return to my country because I have received death threats in my country. Please we need you all to support us. Thank you." Photo by author.

friendly, or even "adequate [to] provide for their safety, security, and medical needs," as the DHS website insisted.[20]

Incarceration as a Human Rights Violation

While the detention of immigrants had been on the rise for a number of years preceding the 2014 influx of Central American refugees and was already being questioned by legal experts for its lack of policy coherence (Gilman 2012), it was at this time that ICE and DHS began arguing that asylum seekers must remain in detention throughout their civil proceedings, because, according to the government, they represent a risk to national security. In bond hearings in immigration court, where judges have the discretion to allow the families to pay a bond and be released while awaiting their hearings, ICE regularly submitted documentation packets that argued that to release the women and children would be a "risk to our national security."[21] Importantly, this argument was not based on any actual risk the individuals themselves posed. Rather, ICE argued that if detainees were freed, it would spark a wave of mass migration, as others would be encouraged to venture to the United States. In other words, women and children already deemed to have a credible fear (and thus a reasonable possibility of winning asylum) were being held in detention for prolonged periods for political reasons having nothing whatsoever to do with them or their cases. Thus, the homeland security state deployed its now well-developed discourse of "potential terrorist immigrants" against women and children who posed no potential harm to the country at all.

In February 2015, in response to a class action lawsuit filed by the ACLU on behalf of women and children detainees, a federal court issued a temporary injunction against the practice of detention as deterrence. The court rejected the government's argument that the detention of women and children was necessary, and in its decision, the court wrote that "the interest proposed by the Government in this case, namely, deterrence of mass migration, is altogether novel" and that the "incantation of the magic word 'national security' without further substantiation is simply not enough to justify significant deprivations of liberty."[22]

ICE responded to the ruling with a new strategy for keeping the women and children in prison. Suddenly, the bond rates shot up to between $5,000 and $10,000, rates Mexican and Central American refugees are unable to pay, effectively ensuring that most detainees would be unable to obtain release. These bonds, which are intended to make sure certain people will comply with later court dates (though studies have shown that asylum seekers have extremely high compliance rates; American Immigration Lawyers Association 2015; Noferi 2015), instead became tools for ensuring the continuation of the government's policy of deterrence by incarceration. The exorbitant bonds sent women into despair, and at least one woman, a Garifuna from Honduras detained with her young daughter, attempted suicide after learning of her unattainable bond rate. Her attorney characterized the high bonds, coming on the heels of previous trauma, as "soul destroying."[23]

This policy of sustained detention violates the rights of women and children refugees under international and domestic law. In recent years, scholars have begun to analyze how prolonged immigration detention itself (not the specific conditions of detention, which I will turn to in a moment) can constitute a human rights violation (Gilman 2012). Gilman lays out in detail how, for "refugees and asylum seekers, the limitations on immigration detention derive from the same human right to liberty guaranteed to all migrants, but also from specific provisions in the refugee treaties" (2012:267).

For example, the United Nations High Commissioner for Refugees characterizes the detention of asylum seekers as "inherently undesirable," and in its interpretation of states' treaty obligations to refugees and asylum seekers, has established a principle "presumption against detention." The Convention Relating to the Status of Refugees establishes that recognized asylum seekers whose cases are pending should not be detained except for a brief period of time to confirm their identity. The UN Working Group on Arbitrary Detention and the UN Rapporteur on the Human Rights of Migrants similarly conclude that the detention of migrants must be a "last resort" (Gilman 2012).

In regard to specifically discretionary (nonmandatory) detention (the category into which the vast majority of women in this study fall), Gilman argues that, because most migrants eligible for release during their proceedings are nevertheless held in detention, for some or all of them, the "statutory regime does not comply with the general principle of international human rights law imposing a presumption against detention" (2012:328). Gilman also addresses the discretionary setting of prohibitively high bonds in order to prolong detention, which runs counter to the presumption against detention and the right to liberty (332). As Gilman amply argues, the United States is in fact bound by international law and treaties, including when these impose human rights limitations on government authority to control immigration.

Although it would perhaps seem obvious, international human rights law also requires that states comply with their own domestic law in regard to migrants (Gilman 2012:273). The detention of women migrants has been deemed inconsistent with U.S. law. Following on the temporary injunction of February 2015, in July of that year the same federal judge ruled that the Obama administration's detention of children and their mothers was a serious violation of the 1997 Flores settlement, and that the families should be released as quickly as possible. Rejecting the administration's arguments for holding the migrants, Judge Dolly M. Gee of the Federal District Court for the Central District of California found that both the Karnes and Dilley detention facilities failed to meet the minimum legal requirements of the Flores settlement for facilities housing children. Gee also found that the authorities had "wholly failed" to provide the "safe and sanitary" conditions required for children. (Remarkably, in spite of this ruling, in May 2016, the Texas Department of Family and Protective Services granted a childcare license to the Karnes County Residential Center. A Texas judge later blocked the licensure, following a lawsuit by Grassroots Leadership and Texas Rural Legal Aid.)[24] Gee's decision was upheld on appeal by the Ninth Circuit in July 2016. Nevertheless, ongoing allegations of abuses and mistreatment of children in detention led the Center for Constitutional Law to file a new motion requesting that the Flores agreement be enforced. In June 2017 Gee found that, among other violations relating to conditions in Customs and Border Protection detention, the government was illegally placing children in unlicensed facilities, had not made continuous efforts to release children, and that children were being detained for excessive periods of time. She ruled that children could not continue to be placed in unlicensed facilities, ordered the government to make individual determinations as to whether each child should continue to be detained, and directed the government to identify and propose a "juvenile coordinator" to report directly to the court regarding the government's compliance with its obligations toward immigrant children in detention, with the threat of an independent observer being assigned in the case of noncompliance.[25]

Thus, the state is clearly not in compliance with domestic law, as a judge has repeatedly ruled. This means that it is also not in compliance with international law and clearly is not meeting the spirit of the international laws and treaties to which it is beholden. The conditions of detention and the prolonged detention of women and children in immigration detention facilities are a violation of their human rights.

Humanitarian Considerations: Women's Mental and Physical Health

The harm being generated by these human rights violations is obvious to anyone visiting the facilities. For the women I spoke with, the condition of being incarcerated has led to deepened emotional trauma, and often their desperation to be free is palpable, in spite of the bright paint on the cellblocks and the crocheting and zumba classes they are offered. This is as true for the women in Hutto as for the women in Dilley and Karnes. Even as women in the family facilities anguish over their children, who lose weight, become listless and despondent, are deprived of medicine and other medical care, and suffer symptoms of PTSD, anxiety, and depression from being in prolonged detention, women in Hutto worry constantly over children with whom they have little or no contact and whose fates are not in their control. The separation causes grief and sorrow that affects, in some cases dramatically, their emotional and physical well-being. Estrella anguished over the newborn baby she left behind in Guatemala. Candelaria, whose story I present later in this chapter, spent over a year in detention, devastated that her daughter was in the care of friends, a separation she had gone to tremendous lengths to avoid.

Ysinia's depression deepened by the day as she agonized over the fates of her children in Guatemala. Women in all the detention facilities bear not only the solitude and shackles of incarceration but also the anxiety of being sent back at a moment's notice to the very violence they had fled. While visiting women in detention, I watched their psychological and physical states deteriorate as their incarcerations dragged on and they waited for their cases to be adjudicated. The women's stories bear witness to the extraordinary challenges to the human spirit caused by detention. Human rights organizations such as Human Rights First have long documented the negative mental and physical health impacts of detention on children and mothers: "Leading pediatricians, physicians, and social workers have found that detention, even for short periods of time, can lead to depression, anxiety, behavioral regressions, and suicidality."[26] This view is supported by the expert witness testimony of Luis Zayas, dean of the School of Social Work at the University of Texas, Austin, who worked with women and children in Karnes:

> Detention has had serious and long-lasting impacts on the psychological health and well-being of the families I interviewed at Karnes. This was evident even though the families I interviewed had been detained at Karnes for a relatively limited period of time—i.e., two to three weeks. In general, mothers and children showed high levels of anxiety—especially separation anxiety for the children—symptoms of depression, and feelings of despair. Children showed signs that detention had caused developmental regression, such as reversion to breastfeeding, and major psychiatric disorders, including suicidal ideation. Teenagers showed signs of depression and anxiety and, in some cases, major depressive disorders. The impacts of detention are exacerbated by the fact that families have already experienced serious trauma in their home countries and in the course of their journey to the United States.[27]

As Zayas's testimony suggests, the emotional and psychological wounds caused by detention build on and exacerbate the trauma they have already experienced in the violent events in their home countries and the perilous passage through Mexico. Zayas continues, "The psychological traumas experienced by these mothers and children—in their home countries, during their travel to the United States, and upon their detention in the United States—will require years of mental health services to alleviate. Moreover, the ongoing stress, despair, and uncertainty of detention—for even a relatively brief period of time—specifically compromises the children's intellectual and cognitive development and contributes to the development of chronic illness in ways that may be irreversible. Detention at Karnes puts children at risk of recurrent and distressing memories, nightmares, dissociative reactions, prolonged psychological distress, and negative alterations in cognition."[28]

While Zayas focuses specifically on children, the recurrent nightmares, distressing memories, and dissociative reactions were also clearly observable in women detainees, and they regularly spoke of insomnia, anxiety attacks, and headaches. Estrella visibly trembled and easily broke into tears; Ysina complained of headaches and sleepless nights and fear. Digna believes that many of her medical issues were a result of severe depression tied to being incarcerated: "Since I arrived [in Hutto] I was sick, I fell into a depression . . . I spent all the time crying because I had never before been a prisoner. I wanted to die." The vast array of ailments Digna suffered were also clearly tied to her emotional deterioration. Needless to say, once released, women rarely get the "years of mental health services [required] to alleviate" their conditions.

At the most fundamental level, human rights law says civil detention is a violation of the right to liberty for people who have committed no criminal act. Being deprived of one's liberty has a real and tangible effect on women's mental health, and their desperation mounts with time. As the social worker Olivia López said in her testimony, "It might look like they're having fun playing soccer, but that's certainly not the narrative of their lives," she said. "They know where they're at. They know they're in a prison. They know they can't leave."[29] Her comments were reminiscent of the sentiments voiced by the immigrant advocate on the tour of the Karnes facility, months before it would be deemed a family detention center, when he suggested that the only way to make the facility truly kinder and gentler would be to install an exit. Without one that the women can access, they are not free. That loss of freedom has devastating effects on their psyches and violates their human rights.

Abuse in Detention

As the abuses in Hutto and Karnes demonstrate, detention creates the conditions of possibility for further abuses by generating a captive population vulnerable to them. Multiple reports in recent years have documented human rights abuses in immigration detention, including rape and other sexual abuse (National Prison Rape Elimination Commission 2009) and a lack of adequate health care (Amnesty International 2009). According to documents obtained by the ACLU (2012), there have been nearly two hundred reports of abuse of detained women since 2007. A Human Rights Watch report in

2010 chronicled numerous incidents and allegations of sexual assault, abuse, or harassment from across the ICE detention system, involving more than fifty detainee victims. In 2018 an investigative journalist at the *New York Times* obtained ICE records of reports of sexual abuse in ICE custody between 2014 and 2017: there were 1,310.[30] An investigation by a national advocacy organization, Community Initiatives for Visiting Immigrants in Confinement, determined that more complaints were submitted against ICE than any other DHS component agency. In their investigation, in addition to 1,016 complaints of sexual abuse or assault, they found 402 complaints of "coerced sexual contact," 196 complaints of "sexual harassment," and 380 complaints of "physical or sexual abuse" filed by people in detention.[31] The investigation also demonstrated that even when ICE knows about complaints, it rarely investigates. The number of reported cases almost certainly does not come close to capturing the extent of the problem, because victims of abuse in detention face a range of obstacles and disincentives to reporting (Community Initiatives for Visiting Immigrants in Confinement 2017; Human Rights Watch 2010). The state is at times directly responsible for creating the legal conditions that facilitate such violence against women. For example, the Department of Justice recently argued that immigrant detention centers should be excluded from the application of the Prison Rape Elimination Act, which establishes standards for preventing, detecting, and responding to sexual abuse. Apparently, once interpellated by the state as terrorists and national security risks, immigrant women no longer merit protection from sexual abuse. The expansion of the Prison Rape Elimination Act to immigrant detention centers had to be established by a presidential act under the Obama administration, which was then in the process of "nicing-up" some of the detention centers following lawsuits against DHS. However, the act merely called on DHS to create its own standards for protecting immigrants from abuses, leaving many doubting whether it would have any effect at all.[32] The inspector general's investigation into the alleged abuses at Karnes provides evidence of the weaknesses inherent in having the state investigate itself.

A recent report on addressing sexual violence in detention highlighted the fact that the most marginalized detainees are also the most vulnerable to abuse (Rothstein and Stannow 2009). The Department of Justice report on sexual victimization in prisons and jails found that the highest rates of victimization were among people with high levels of psychological distress (Beck, et. al. 2012). Women who have been multiply subject to violence enter detention in a vulnerable state due to their emotional distress, and this renders them further vulnerable.

While all women are at risk of such violence, Indigenous women are at even greater risk, particularly if they do not speak Spanish, which isolates them and makes it virtually impossible for them to report. Indigenous women tend to be isolated even within the larger detainee population. A number of the women I worked with expressed this sense of isolation. This is attributable not only to both language incompatibility and communication issues, but also to larger issues of race that are transposed onto the detention context. In other words, non-Indigenous women may view Indigenous women as "different" and culturally distant from themselves. This isolation may render them more vulnerable, as they are not only unlikely to report to authorities, but also less likely than others to share the information with anyone at all because of their isolation.

Indigenous Language and Vulnerability

Candelaria left her home in Todos Santos, Guatemala, seeking a better life in the United States. She joined relatives in Washington State and began work harvesting plants. Her daughter was born there the following year. When her daughter was two, Candelaria was apprehended in a workplace raid by ICE. When she failed to appear for a court date, she was ordered deported. With a deportation order against her, she lived for several years in fear of being apprehended and deported without her daughter. Finally, she decided it was better to return to Guatemala than to risk such a separation. There, she began a relationship with a man who quickly became abusive. His violence was so severe that Candelaria bears a number of visible scars on her face and head from his beatings. Finally, Candelaria put her U.S. citizen daughter on a plane to Seattle and undertook the long journey overland.

Candelaria's journey was long and difficult, and it included being kidnapped and held for ransom by a cartel in Reynosa, grabbed off the streets minutes after arriving there. Fortunately, having lived in the United States previously, she had people she could call to get the money. When she was released and finally made it to the border and attempted to enter the United States, she was abandoned by her coyote in the desert when the Border Patrol appeared and her group was forced to scatter. After wandering lost for two days, terrified and without food or water, she was apprehended by the Border Patrol. When she expressed fear of returning to Guatemala, she was thrown into immigration detention and ended up at the T. Don Hutto facility. She was extremely grief-stricken about being separated from her young daughter, the very thing she had been attempting to avoid by returning to Guatemala in the first place. She was insecure about her Spanish, which, despite her time in the United States, was still not strong because she has lived in an immigrant community in which everyone spoke her native language. She had learned from women at the detention center that if she failed to pass her credible fear interview, she would be deported to Guatemala. With her entire future, and especially her ability to get back to her daughter, riding on it, she requested an interpreter in the Mam language for her asylum interview, her right under the law. That decision would cost her eight months of separation from her child, during which she languished in detention, as her annoyed deportation officer harassed her to "give up" and just do her interview in Spanish.

As Candelaria's story reflects, being a speaker of an Indigenous language can profoundly increase one's vulnerability to multiple forms of violence. She requested a Mam interpreter, only to find that it took months to procure one, making her deportation officer hostile to her and prolonging her detention significantly, thus inflicting the worst pain on her she could imagine, separation from her only child. Estrella suffered a similar process, waiting over a year in detention for an interpreter to be found. Notably, both women speak Mam, one of the most prevalent Mayan languages in the United States and one of the four Mayan languages for which an interpreter should have been available.[33] This raises the unconfirmable suspicion that the delay was partially punitive, rather than a practical necessity. The U.S. government is obligated to ensure that Indigenous-language speakers have meaningful access to federal programs and activities. Customs and Border Protection and ICE both have plans in place to accommodate people with limited English proficiency. However, according to the family detention advocacy coalition CARA,[34] such plans are inadequate and their implementation does "not even provide minimal protection for non-English speakers."[35] Even the U.S. Government Accountability Office has criticized DHS's limited English proficiency engagement in 2010.[36] In the CARA complaint, the organization alleges that DHS's "failure to correctly identify the primary language spoken by Indigenous asylum seekers, along with its practice of conducting interrogations in a language these women do not fully understand, has led to the erroneous deportation of families seeking protection in the United States, returning them to life-threatening situations in their home countries."[37]

Thus, Indigenous women migrants whose primary language is not English or Spanish are rendered vulnerable in multiple ways. They are less likely than others to be fairly treated in their asylum process due to a lack of access to effective communication about the threats that they face (discussed further in chapter 5). This can result in negative outcomes for their cases and deportation into settings where they are in further danger. If they request an interpreter, they may experience prolonged waits in detention. While in detention, they experience isolation from other women and suffer the corresponding psychological impact of loneliness, as well as a lack of access to the informal information networks that other women provide. They may be even more vulnerable than others to gender violence such as sexual harassment or assault by authorities because of their isolation and lack of ability to report. In all of these regards, Indigenous women experience the migration process differently from others and are multiply *vulneradas*.

Racism

Indigenous women experience racism in their incarceration, both from guards in the facilities and, sadly, though perhaps not surprisingly, from fellow detainees. Mexico, Guatemala, and Honduras are countries that, as we have seen, are characterized by strong and enduring racial structures and ideologies. These are not checked at the border when women migrate, and mestiza women regularly talk down to and make racist assumptions about Indigenous women in the centers. Several women mentioned feeling increased isolation because they were "different" from the other women, and they also reported women laughing at them (perhaps not mean-spiritedly, but hurtfully nonetheless) because their clothes were far too large for their small frames. Digna, in particular, as an Indigenous Afro-descendant, found that the other women referred to her as *la negra*, which she found to be deprecating. She also experienced racism from the CCA guards, particularly those she identified as Chicano, whom she felt treated her differently from mestizo Central Americans, possibly because they carried a U.S. racial imaginary in which blacks are understood differently from Latinos. She believes she was the first singled out for punishment during the strikes in part because of this racism, as well as her general poor health, which made her a "problem."

Erasure

Another form of violence is inflicted on Indigenous women when they enter the bowels of the homeland security state through the immigration detention system. Their identity and status as Indigenous people are taken from them. Because "qualifying" as Indigenous in the United States is largely premised, despite the multiple and serious problems this entails, on belonging to a group that the federal government recognizes as a tribe, Indigenous people from Latin America cannot and will not ever fully qualify as Indigenous once they have entered the United States. From the time they cross the border, they are engaged by the state only as "Mexican nationals" or "Guatemalan nationals," effectively erasing their Indigenous identity.[38] Not simply a matter of classification, this erasure fundamentally affects their status as political subjects before the state and disempowers them from making claims based on their identity. Notably, the erasure of Indigenous migrants' identity as Indigenous people is one in a long series of technologies used by settler states to eliminate Indigenous people. Indigenous erasure, of course, has taken many forms in the settler state, including the settler states of Mexico, Guatemala, and Honduras. These include, but are not limited to, notions of blood quantum (rendering each generation smaller); assimilationism (turning Indians into white people); manipulation of census data (literally not counting Indians, or setting definitional criteria to limit Indigenous identification); land allotment (making collective Indians into individual landowning farmers); agrarian reform (making Indians into peasants); and compulsory urbanization through a variety of means, ranging from relocation policies to land lost to megadevelopment projects (turning Indians into city folk). In the current double move of rendering them "nationals" of their home countries, Indigenous women are erased as Indigenous and reraced as immigrants, and thus criminal or terrorist elements. This move is important because it is precisely what allows their treatment to be acceptable, both in a legal sense (they are not Indigenous and therefore do not qualify for sovereignty or a special relationship to the state) and in a human rights sense (they do not deserve fair treatment because they are potentially dangerous to us). Further, by defining them exclusively as nationals of another state and not as Indigenous people belonging to Indigenous nations, the sovereignty of the settler state (both the United States and the home state) is affirmed.

IN THIS CHAPTER, I have examined how the state interpellates migrants through its laws and policies in the United States, and the ways these interpellations do violence to people's physical and emotional well-being. In particular, I consider how Indigenous women migrants experience the state differently from other migrants who undergo immigration policing, detention, and deportation, because of their race and gender and are multiply *vulneradas* by the neoliberal homeland security state (Gonzales 2013).

The emergence and consolidation of the U.S. carceral state has been such an important political dynamic in recent decades that political scientists have argued that it "rivals in significance the expansion and contraction of the welfare state in the postwar period" (Gottschalk 2008:236) and constitutes a "durable shift in governing authority" (Orren and Skowronek 2004:123) in which the state began to exercise vast new controls over millions of people. The rise of the carceral state is inseparable from the rise of neoliberalism—as Gilmore suggests, it is precisely the rise of neoliberalism that necessitated new forms of governance and control (Gilmore 2007). This rise in mass incarceration is not color-blind or gender-neutral. People of color are incarcerated at much higher rates than whites (Alexander 2012; Lytle Hernández 2017), and, as Crenshaw has argued, "the structural and political dimensions of gender violence and mass incarceration are linked in multiple ways" (2012:1418).

While this carceral control is directed at immigrants, that should not obscure its settler character. All too often, immigrants are positioned against Indigenous people as fundamentally opposite subjects in relation to the state: a "nation of immigrants" in principle accommodates arrivals while harboring a fundamental tension with original, nonimmigrant peoples. However, as historian David Chang eloquently framed the question in a recent Facebook post, "We watch the American settler state under Trump reaching a moment of brutal clarity as it sweeps away liberal fictions of 'a nation of immigrants,' fictions that are torn up and discarded like so many tipis at Standing Rock. A settler colonial nation, founded on dispossession, is not a nation of immigrants." Chang suggests that immigration policy has always been a "brutal process meant to engineer a particular kind of settler nation on Native land." He notes, "Slave trade. Chinese exclusion. Bracero program. Mass deportation. These, too, are immigration policy. So the brutalization of the migrant is structurally inseparable from the dispossession of the Native."[39] It is also clear from Chang's examples—all of which were responses to changing labor needs—that it is fundamentally inseparable from capitalism. Of course, the "particular kind of settler nation on Native land" that the settler state wishes to engineer is a *white* settler state. This is why race (and racism/white supremacy) continues to structure power in the United States, as well as the other states discussed so far. Thus, for the white settler capitalist state, carcerality is a tool of control to manage its ongoing occupation (Lytle Hernandez 2018). Raced and gendered carcerality facilitates the management of settler sovereignty and territoriality through the control of remaining Indigenous peoples and invading nonwhite potential settlers, together with the African American population produced by the colonially facilitated, capitalism-necessitated practice of slavery, a population that must be maintained in a perpetual state of incomplete enfranchisement and citizenship. In the settler state, therefore, the Indigenous migrant occupies a double subject position: "those who pose a risk by remaining" and "those who pose a risk by invading." The women whose stories I consider in this book, Indigenous women migrants, embody all of these vulnerabilities as they are subject to multiple and overlapping forces of carceral control as women, as Indigenous people, and as migrants.

In the last chapter, I considered how these forces play out in the context of the neoliberal multicriminalism at work in Mexico and Central America. In this chapter, the focus has been on the U.S. state and how its laws and policies deploy similar forces against women. However, my point is not that in Latin America illegality reigns, while in the United States the state confines itself to legal means of control (even if by manipulating law and policy). While I am concerned with the ways that law and legal frameworks serve to uphold state power and facilitate state control and subject-making, I am equally asserting that U.S. law and policy toward immigrants is illegal in various respects (with my particular focus here on asylum seekers), as it violates both domestic and international law and sidesteps responsibility by outsourcing its policing and carceral functions to the private sector (in ways that generate huge profits). In this sense (as well as by enabling markets for illegal goods and perpetuating conditions of impunity for trafficking in the United States, discussed elsewhere in this book), the United States is also part of neoliberal multicriminalism.

But I want to come back to the concept of the settler capitalist state in order to draw the lens out from the current moment and emphasize, again, the continuity of the overarching structures that generate these vulnerabilities, and the particular place of human caging within them (Lytle Hernández 2017). As I have noted throughout, the ideologies of race and gender that play a role in rendering women vulnerable in this context are settler-generated ideologies that have persisted through time just as the settler state has, and while they are deployed differently in different contexts and phases of capitalism, they continue the same work of controlling and managing populations that pose a risk to settler-state power. Indeed, the immigration prisons of the neoliberal multicriminal era serve as the space for the settler state, through law and policy, to perform its sovereignty, asserting its right to be and to rule in this territory.

In the next chapter, I will turn to an examination of how these forces play out in the United States and Latin America once women gain their freedom from detention.

CHAPTER FIVE

Beyond Detention

Undocumented Dangers and Deportability

Rosa left her home in Guerrero, Mexico, after her husband disappeared. He had been forced to carry drugs for the local cartel and one day he did not return home after a trip outside the town. She tried to report his disappearance to police, who had little interest in pursuing the matter. One went so far as to warn her to be quiet about the disappearance if she did not want to suffer a similar fate. After she traveled to the state capital to seek further assistance in locating her husband, a neighbor reported seeing armed men outside her home. Four months pregnant with her first child and afraid for her and her child's lives, she fled to the United States, where she had a brother living in Texas. She was caught crossing the border with a false ID and deposited in Reynosa, where she was quickly picked up by cartel gangs and held for ransom, but her brother was able to pay for her release. When she attempted to cross again, she was apprehended, and when she begged them not to send her back, stating that she was afraid for her unborn child's life, she was held in detention, eventually ending up in the Hutto facility. Rosa was deemed to have a credible fear of return to Mexico and was released on bond pending her asylum proceedings after her brother presented a letter stating that he would be financially responsible for her. Before her release, she expressed extreme anxiety about what would happen next. Would she stand any chance of success in her legal case? She did not have money for a lawyer, and she already owed her brother the money he had paid for her ransom and her bond. How would he, a much older brother she hadn't seen in years who had a family of his own to support, treat her and her newborn when they were his dependents? How would she work? How would they survive?

We have seen that Indigenous women are vulnerable to violence and human rights violations at home, in migration, and in U.S. detention. Their vulnerability does not end with release from detention. For many, their detention ends with injustice in the immigration system and a forced return to the very violence they risked their lives to get away from. For others, like Rosa, it means the vulnerability of being in the United States with temporary residency status, without permission to work, and in fear of the outcome of their cases, which can take up to two years or more if they are not detained. Recall the women abused by the Corrections Corporation of America officer at Hutto as he drove them from their detention facility to airports and bus stations upon their release. They were not even an hour out of the facility before they were being abused, a crime the officer surely believed they would not report. In this chapter, we consider Rosa's experience and return to the stories of Virgilia, Candelaria, and Hilaria to explore their experiences post-detention.

Deportation

Virgilia was apprehended by the U.S. Border Patrol after her pollero abandoned her in the desert, shouting racist insults as he went. In custody, Border Patrol agents attempted to threaten and cajole her into accepting voluntary departure to Mexico, but Virgilia refused. When she told them she was afraid to return to her country, she was placed in political asylum proceedings and pitched into the vast immigration detention system, eventually winding up in the Hutto facility. Less than two months later, an asylum officer who interviewed her only by video conference, in Spanish, deemed her not to have a "credible fear." Despite the clear physical evidence of her severe abuse, which included a twice-broken clavicle and visible scars on her face and back, Virgilia was deported.

Virgilia returned to San Cristobal de las Casas after her deportation. I met her there briefly in the summer of 2014. She was living with her children and was very happy to be reunited with them. However, she was struggling to support herself and them and also to repay the large sum of money she had borrowed to pay her coyote. She was also nervous and constantly afraid that the children's father, her former abuser, would reappear and kill her or take the children from her. However, when I asked if she would consider migrating again, she replied, "No, nothing could make me. I still have terrible memories of what happened to me. If I have to die, I would rather die here, and not alone in the desert or in a detention cell. Besides, even if I made it back to the other side, they will never let me stay over there." Her direct answer seemed to acknowledge her state of vulnerability anywhere, even as it recognized the violence of her journey and her deportation. It also reflects the violence of the immigration process: she saw no reason to hope that even if she survived another journey and made it into the United States, there would be a path for her to remain legally (despite what should have been a strong asylum case), and she felt that she would always be vulnerable to deportation.

The threat of deportation plagues many migrants, even those who have been in the United States for years. As we saw in Candelaria's story, she had been living in undocumented status in the States for a number of years when she became a victim of a workplace ICE raid. Unable to afford a lawyer and afraid to attend her hearing, she was ordered to be deported and was living with a constant threat that she would be detained and sent back to Guatemala without her U.S. citizen daughter. That fear was enough to cause her to self-deport, taking her daughter with her. The implications for women's vulnerability are significant and are discussed further in this chapter. For the many women who are actually deported, their journey ends in a final, state-sponsored act of violence — one that returns them to the very dangers they fled in the first place.

Deportations have been on the rise since the mid-1990s, but like detention, they accelerated in the post-9/11 period. The Obama administration famously (or infamously) deported more immigrants than any prior administration, leading the president to be dubbed "deporter in chief" by immigration advocates. As of 2015, more than 2.5 million undocumented people had been deported by immigration authorities since President Barack Obama took office in 2009. This total exceeds that of the two terms of his predecessor, George W. Bush, by half a million people, and led critics to refer to the period as the Obama administration's "five-year deportation spree."[1] An additional 450,000 were deported in 2016 (Department of Homeland Security [DHS] 2016), bringing the Obama administration's total close to nearly 3 million. Obama continued down the path opened by Bush following 9/11, when the criminalization of immigrants was set in motion. The Immigration and Naturalization Service was dissolved and reformulated as Immigration and Customs Enforcement (ICE) under the DHS and linked to the Secure Communities Act, reflecting the new understanding of immigrants as terrorists and criminals (discussed in more detail in the previous chapter). Accordingly, Obama justified the high number of deportations by arguing that those deported were criminals, not law-abiding people. In 2014, as he presented a new memo on priorities for immigration enforcement, he said that immigration officials would make it a priority to deport immigrants who had committed serious crimes. "We're going to keep focusing enforcement resources on actual threats to our security. Felons, not families. Criminals, not children. Gang members, not a mom who's working hard to provide for her kids" (White House Office of the Press Secretary 2014).

However, critics consistently reported that the numbers told a different story. For example, one news story stated, "The Department of Homeland Security reported that it removed and returned over 450,000 people in 2016. Of this number, 85 percent were people caught crossing the border without authorization. Fewer than 8 percent of these deportees were felons or accused of being in a street gang. Even if one just looks at ICE administrative arrests in the interior of the country, and ignores the people caught crossing the border, less than 9 percent of these people had felonies or were in street gangs."[2] The Marshall Project, which examined data from over three hundred thousand deportations that followed Obama's speech, reported, "The majority—roughly sixty percent—were of immigrants with no criminal conviction or whose only crime was immigration-related, such as illegal entry or re-entry. Twenty-one percent were convicted of nonviolent crimes other than immigration. Fewer than twenty percent had potentially violent convictions, such as an assault, DUI, or weapons offenses."[3] Further, critics suggest that Latino, Afro-Caribbean, and Muslim immigrants disproportionately suffered enforcement, "reflecting the racial profiling to which these populations are subject in the criminal justice, immigration, and national security systems."[4]

In any case, the claim to be deporting only criminals seems remarkably incongruent with the reinstitution of family detention, which the Obama administration had undertaken just months before the "felons, not families," speech, as well as the open policy asserting that women and children refugees posed a "national security threat" if not detained as a deterrent to other potential refugees. Further, in conjunction with his emergency appropriations request that summer to expand detention beds for families, Obama asked that DHS be granted the authority to "fast-track" procedures for the screening and deportation of all unaccompanied minors. Immigrant advocacy and human rights organizations, alarmed by the fast-tracking of all refugees at the border, began to sound alarm bells.[5] Human Rights Watch, in a report entitled, *"You Don't Have Rights Here": US Border Screening and Returns of Central Americans to Risk of Serious Harm*, writes, "At the US-Mexico border, US immigration officers issue deportation orders to unauthorized migrants in accelerated processes known as 'expedited removal' or 'reinstatement of removal.' These processes include rapid-fire screening for a migrant's fear of persecution or torture upon return to their home country or an intention to apply for asylum. As detailed in this report, this cursory screening is failing to effectively identify people fleeing serious risks to their lives and safety. . . . The U.S. government's rapid-fire screening of unauthorized migrants at the border is *sending Central Americans back to the risk of serious harm*" (2014b:1, emphasis mine). That assertion has been substantiated by several investigative journalists and at least one academic study, which found that people who were returned to their countries in expedited removal or another form of deportation in some cases indeed met their deaths. An investigative report by the *Guardian* and various other news sources have cited the research of Elizabeth Kennedy, who compiled a comprehensive list of U.S. deportees murdered on their return to Central America since January 2014, based on local newspaper reports. Kennedy's research identified forty-five such cases in El Salvador, three in Guatemala, and thirty-five in Honduras. The *Guardian* quotes Kennedy: "These figures tell us that the U.S. is returning people to their deaths in violation of national and international law."[6] After his fear was deemed "not credible" and he was deported, Digna's partner, Marlon, suffered this fate, murdered by the very gang that had killed his father and brother and had previously threatened him.

Indigenous women are at particular risk of deportation due to their language and cultural differences. Illiteracy is high among Indigenous women, particularly in Guatemala, where nearly half of Indigenous women do not read or write (UN Women 2011) and the percentage of Indigenous women who are monolingual in the Indigenous language is relatively high. If they are not literate or are not fluent Spanish speakers, these women may be coerced into signing papers, such as voluntary departure forms, that they do not understand. Lack of literacy complicates Indigenous women's understanding of the entire asylum process, and they can easily make a mistake or miss something important that can result in deportation. Both language and cultural differences may also make it difficult for women to present their narratives in the form necessary in order for an asylum officer or immigration judge to deem it credible. Because Indigenous narrative forms are often nonchronological and narrative conventions in most Indigenous languages are quite distinct from those of English, their rendering of the story may seem confusing or even untruthful. Relatedly, because levels of violence against Indigenous women are high, PTSD-related memory gaps may also make it difficult for them to tell their stories in a manner that will gain them a grant of asylum. Deportation is a real danger for Indigenous women migrants; whether "fast-tracked" to removal by Customs and Border Protection, "expedited" to it following a credible fear interview like Virgilia, or deported following an unsuccessful asylum case, women who have fled and are returned into violence are often at even more serious risk than when they left.

Indigenous women's vulnerability to deportation is, once again, intersectional and structural: as Indigenous women, they are dark-skinned, even within the larger category of Latin American immigrants, and as such are more likely to experience racial profiling. If their Spanish skills are not strong, they are less likely than others to be able to convey their fear to a Customs and Border Protection officer, sound credible to an asylum office, or reasonably and convincingly tell their stories and respond to questions from immigration judges and government attorneys. Almost invariably impoverished, they lack the resources for an attorney, an advantage that would make them four times more likely to be released from detention, eleven "times more likely to seek relief such as asylum, and twice as likely to obtain the relief they sought" (Eagly and Shafer 2016). On top of all that, they are subject to policies of "prevention by detention" and "prevention by deportation" (to complement De Leon's "prevention by deterrence"), in which refugees fleeing violence, and particularly women and children, are used as a tool to deter further refugee arrivals. In this, their gender and status as mothers render them doubly vulnerable. Thus, many women wind up removed: like Rosa, they are "returned into the arms of cartels,"[7] or, like Virgilia, deported, after their legitimate fear is deemed noncredible although it is fairly clear that they do not stand a chance of safe haven. Or they face the fate of Candelaria, who was subject to an ICE raid on a workplace filled with Indigenous workers, leading to a deportation order that motivated her to return to Guatemala and to a violent relationship there, then again into the arms of ICE, where her fate was to be decided. She may join the ranks of one-quarter of all deportees who are cleaved from their U.S. citizen children.[8] These deportations do not just render women vulnerable to new risks; they constitute a form of violence against them and potentially a violation of their human rights as well.

Deportability

Marisol, traumatized by years of abuse, took a machete to the stranger who raped her, and then fled to the United States, fearing the police would arrest her rather than her rapist. She traveled on a bus and was able to cross Mexico without incident—something few women I have talked to would be able to say. However, once she was across the border and in a U.S. border town, a man followed her out of a convenience store. She ran; he chased her. Marisol believed he was a person who preyed on undocumented migrants and likely intended to rape her. She managed to evade him by hiding in a clothing store, but when she came out, she was so terrified that he would reappear and harm her that she turned herself in to the Border Patrol. She thought she would be safe in immigration custody. She learned differently when sent to one of the worst facilities in the state of Texas, where guards repeatedly verbally assaulted and humiliated her and other detainees.

The vast majority of Indigenous women, once they have left their home countries, enter the vulnerable realm of the undocumented, since few are able to obtain visas to legally immigrate. We have seen some of the outcomes of that vulnerability for Central American women in Mexico. In just one example, consider the array of abusers who preyed on Marleny's vulnerability as an undocumented child, resulting in her being raped twice by two different men. The myriad relationships she became involved in, and the constant evaluations she was required to make of offers of protection, as well as who and what represents a risk at any moment in time, reflect what Vogt refers to as "the intimate, embodied and affective dimensions of mobility for unauthorised Central American migrants in Mexico" (Vogt 2016:366). As Vogt analyzes, "While in transit, migrants become implicated within the violence of local and transnational economies of smuggling, organised crime, kidnapping and securitisation. At the same time, migrants engage intimate economies of exchange, kinship and care as they negotiate their movements and their lives" (2016:366). Marleny struggled to negotiate these complexities and understand her location within them, forming relationships repeatedly with people who initially helped her but later betrayed her. The loss of her son, a brutal violence perpetrated against her by her rapist's parents, probably could not and would not have been committed if she had not been undocumented. Her status was wielded against her to ensure that she would not seek redress. Others were also made vulnerable by their undocumented status. Marisol felt so vulnerable as an undocumented immigrant that she turned herself over to Border Patrol. We also saw how women in the detention system in the United States were more vulnerable to abuse for a variety of reasons, including fear of reporting, inability to report because of a lack of language skills, and a lack of knowledge of their rights. Following on all of these ways that women are *vulneradas*, deportation becomes an additional harm, putting them at new (or old) risk. This is true both in a practical sense, as it was for Virgilia, and in a *potential* sense, as women's state of "deportability" creates new vulnerabilities.

The Border Patrol separated Marleny from her brother. They were interrogated and, in Marleny's words, "treated like animals." Border Patrol officers accused them of lying and tried to make them admit that they were not related. They accused Marleny's brother of being a criminal and told Marleny that she was a prostitute who only came "to suck the oxygen from this country." Marleny and her brother didn't give in to the pressure, insisting that they were fleeing violence and that if returned to Honduras, they would be killed. Eventually, they were released and given a paper with a court date. Marleny had no idea what it was: she did not read English and nothing was explained to her. She missed her court date and has lived without documents in the United States ever since.

Marleny was released without bond, and it is unclear whether she was ever in asylum proceedings. Most of the women I met had been in either the Hutto or the Karnes facility and were eventually released on bond (or, on rare occasions, without bond, as in Estrella's case) following a successful credible fear interview. Usually, their bond is set fairly high, then reduced at a bond hearing. In order to get the bond reduced, they must provide a permanent address where they will reside and a letter from a relative or other person stating that they will provide for them (asylum applicants are not granted work permits). Some women, like Estrella and Hilaria, are accepted into the local immigrant shelter Casa Marianella, which has been housing immigrants since the 1980s. Having grown to three houses, the shelter provides a separate residence for families consisting of women and children, Posada Esperanza. Others travel to family or friends, often in other states. If they go to another state, their attorney, if they have one, may file a petition to move their immigration cases to a closer venue or may tell them they are responsible for getting an attorney in their new location and then filing a change of venue. If they do not have an attorney, they are responsible for filing the petition for the change or returning to San Antonio for their hearing. When a case venue is moved, they are notified by U.S. postal service at the address they gave upon bonding out. Cases of detained people (and minors) take priority in the scheduling backlog, so many women released from detention will have their cases set several years out, with variance by region. If they move and fail to update their address with U.S. Citizenship and Immigration Services, the agency of DHS that administers and oversees naturalization and immigration systems, they may not receive important information about when and where their hearings will take place.[9] Failure to appear at any hearing results in an order of deportation against them, as well as revocation (forfeiture) of the bond. Many women, like Marleny, are released without a real understanding of what is happening. Several women in Hutto told me that they had "won" their cases after a successful credible fear interview, and that they were being released. It was very clear they did not understand that they had simply passed a first step in the process and would need to continue their case in court once released. Undoubtedly, some women coming out of these facilities, like Marleny, fail to appear on their court date out of a lack of understanding of the process and are ordered deported. Naturally, this is more likely to happen to Indigenous women whose Spanish is limited or who are illiterate because they cannot read the paperwork that is provided to them.

A number of aspects of this process bear further consideration in relation to generating women's vulnerability, particularly the threat of deportation. Women who apply for asylum after they are apprehended by immigration enforcement are already in removal (deportation) proceedings. Their asylum application is considered "defensive"—it is a defense against removal. They are repeatedly informed that they are in removal proceedings, leading the women to feel vulnerable to summary deportation at any time, even if this is not the case. Bonds, even when they are on the lower end of the scale, are a great deal of money for the migrant women, who generally arrive with nothing. (The minimum bond is $1,500 and went as high as $30,000 in the period when ICE was utilizing bonds to keep refugee women in detention as a deterrent. Most bonds I saw were in the $3,000 to $5,000 range.) This means that family members or others must loan the bond money, creating obligations that can generate future vulnerabilities, especially when coupled with letters of support or maintenance from family members. For example, a brother or uncle who has provided a bond and a letter saying he will support the woman may hold considerable power over her. Women who have no resources to hire an attorney may not file their change of venue request, since they are impeded by language and the complexity of the process, and may be financially or otherwise unable to return for the hearing. If this happens, a deportation order will be issued, making them deportable at any time. If they do file a petition to change venue, but move without updating their address, they may not know of their hearing when it happens, with a similar outcome. This also creates a layer of vulnerability because they cannot easily move away from a potentially abusive family member if that address is where they expect their immigration papers to arrive. In short, the immigration process itself generates structural components of women's vulnerability.

Shortly after Marleny arrived at her brother's house in Texas, there was an incident in which her brother became angry with her and beat her. Marleny became very depressed. She felt very alone in this alien place, but knew she could now never return to Mexico because of the drug trafficker.

Marleny met her future husband through her brother. For the first year, their relationship was fine. He was undocumented, too, but had been in the States a long time. He spoke English and knew how to manage things better than Marleny. She didn't love him, but she did not want to be alone, or dependent on her brother, and he provided some companionship and support. She was only sixteen. By the second year of the relationship, when her daughter was born, he had begun to be jealous and controlling. He drank a lot and became violent. By the third year, she felt like a prisoner in her own home. He wouldn't allow her to work or talk to the neighbors. When they went out, he clutched her hand as if she were going to get away. She was frightened of his violence, but even more afraid that he would take her daughter away as he regularly threatened to do. "I couldn't live through that another time," she said.

Women who experience domestic violence, other violence, or exploitation, are often fearful of reporting it to police or seeking other forms of help or support, including medical care for wounds, for fear of disclosing their undocumented status or putting their immigration process in jeopardy (Ray and Silverman 2002; Sokoloff and Dupont 2005). Studies have shown that abusers rely on this reporting gap, knowing they are unlikely to be held accountable (Menjívar and Salcido 2002). Reina, Lohman, and Maldonado, in their study of Latina immigrants and domestic violence, found that "participants indicated that their immigration status was a major factor influencing their help-seeking practices. In this regard three conclusions can be drawn: (a) Abusers use immigration to increase their control and power over their Latina victims, which exacerbate the victims' vulnerability to domestic violence; (b) immigration status influences Latina victims' help-seeking efforts to connect with law enforcement and social service personnel; and (c) although there are policies such as The Violence Against Women Act of 1994 that prevent undocumented Latina victims or those who have unstable residency from deportation, there are still misconceptions among them regarding their unstable residency" (2014:609). Clearly, if this is the case for Latina undocumented women in general, it is also the case for Indigenous women, who are likely to face a language gap that the Latina participants in Reina, Lohman, and Maldonado's study did not.

A variety of structural factors intersect in women's vulnerability to deportation that create this reluctance to report. These include poverty, including both a lack of financial resources for an attorney (who might ensure that they can report abuse without harming their cases) and a financial dependency on family members who in some cases may become abusive. Language is a factor as well, as the law enforcement agencies to which they might report abuse often lack translation services. Many women feel a general lack of trust in law enforcement and government authorities as a result of their experiences at home and in migration, and this is compounded by collaborations between local law enforcement and ICE.[10] Finally, as mentioned earlier, some aspects of immigration law dictate legal and sometimes economic dependency on the abuser (Erez, Adelman, and Gregory 2009).

Significantly, these structural barriers to women's security all hinge on the uncertainties arising from the possibility of deportation. I suggest, following De Genova's 2002 analysis, that the possibility of deportation—the state of deportability—is the key to the state's construction of migrants (and particularly Indigenous women) as vulnerable subjects. De Genova writes, "The disciplinary operation of an apparatus for the everyday production of migrant 'illegality' is never simply intended to achieve the putative goal of deportation. It is deportability, and not deportation per se, that has historically rendered undocumented migrant labor a distinctly disposable commodity" (2002:438). De Genova was writing in 2002, before the post-9/11 changes that included the formation of ICE (which took place the year after his article was published) and the recasting of immigrants as terrorists and criminals. However, his argument takes on new salience in the homeland security era, as discourses of terrorism are deployed against refugee women and children to keep them in a constant state of deportability and thus maintain their vulnerability and exploitability—what Buff (2018) calls "the deportation terror." These discourses also serve to justify and render acceptable to society in general their potential "disposal" through deportation. As crimmigration scholars have demonstrated, criminalizing immigrants creates a legal rational for their exclusion or expulsion (García Hernández 2013; Stumpf 2006). This is what Menjívar and Abrego mean by the "legal violence" that creates structural harm in the "living conditions and experiences of contemporary immigrants in tenuous legal statuses in the United States" (2012:1386–87). By producing deportability through its laws and policies, the United States creates the structural violence that renders Indigenous women and other migrants vulnerable.

However, simply changing policies and laws will not alter the situation. Deportability is necessary not only to maintain capitalist exploitation, but for the construction of settler sovereignty. As Das Gupta argues in a forthcoming work, deportation, which she calls *policing by ejection*, "advances settler colonialism, which depends on territorial control through dispossession, even though on the surface deporting people may appear to be the opposite of settling migrants on Indigenous land. The power to deport advances U.S. legitimacy over a colonized and occupied expanse of land and ocean at the expense of the Indigenous exercise of sovereignty over the space" (Das Gupta forthcoming). Thus deportation and deportability both serve settler sovereignty-making and capitalist exploitation, serving to perpetuate settler-capitalist power and justify its harms. While more gentle policies than those of the current era are possible, the role of deportation and deportability will remain necessary to the settler capitalist state.

Trafficking

> *It is hard to imagine a person more manifestly vulnerable than Estella. At four foot eleven and nineteen years old, she spoke Spanish hesitatingly and often appeared on the verge of tears. Desperate to get out of Hutto, she nearly took voluntary departure. But a sympathetic immigration judge, noting the strength of her case, set her free without bond. She moved into Casa Marianella, the immigrant shelter, but there she often seemed to be in shock, bewildered by her life's whirlwind of assaults and the particularly bizarre twist of having come to rest in the middle of the state of Texas. Less than a month later, she disappeared. Her roommate at the shelter said Estrella had mentioned she might be going to "work" in Washington with "a friend." This seemed odd, since she had reported having no friends in the United States. When people from Casa called the number they found on a tiny piece of paper in her room, a man answered. They asked for Estrella. They heard muffled voices, then Estrella came on the phone, sounding nervous and unnatural. After a moment, the line went dead. That was two years ago. We never heard from Estrella again. We do not know what happened to her, but we believe she was the victim of human traffickers who prey on vulnerable migrants.*

A few years ago, the journal *Foreign Policy* published an article by David Feingold that began, "Judging by news headlines, human trafficking is a recent phenomenon. In fact, the coerced movement of people across borders is as old as the laws of supply and demand. What is new is the volume of the traffic—and the realization that we have done little to stem the tide" (2005:26). Feingold's opening highlighted several significant facts about human trafficking: that it is a market-driven phenomenon, that it has increased dramatically in the current context, and that traffickers can expect relatively little risk of being held accountable for their actions.

In her book on people trafficked into forced labor in the United States, *Life Interrupted*, anthropologist Denise Brennan characterizes trafficking as "migration gone awry" (2014:6) and specifically links it to the pervasive and unchecked labor exploitation in the United States. For Brennan, trafficking is situated along a "continuum of exploitative labor practices" that includes "low pay, no pay, unsafe working conditions, job insecurity, and no clear channels for redress" (2014:12). Although all undocumented migrants and many with temporary visas or work permits are subject to labor exploitation whereby employers leverage migrants' fear of loss of work status or deportation, in trafficking contexts that leveraging takes place to such an extent that individuals have lost their autonomy and have a "compromised ability to walk away" (Brennan 2014:13). While the literature on trafficking often speaks of "modern slavery," this can be misleading because people who have been drawn into forced labor are not shackled or otherwise bound. Brennan continues, "What distinguishes these coerced individuals from their coworkers is that they fear for themselves or their families if they try to leave their abuser. Intimidation works. . . . For some, having no passport, money, contacts in the United States, or even seasonally appropriate clothes shapes their perception of the opportunity and safety of leaving" (2014:13). Not speaking English or even good Spanish and having clothing and an appearance that make you stand out, even from other immigrants, might be added to this list.

The U.S. government estimates that between fifteen thousand and eighteen thousand people are trafficked into the country each year for forced labor or the sex trade (U.S. State Department 2012). Experts agree that the numbers are likely far higher, since the secretive nature of the crime makes it difficult to track. While estimates vary, all agree that more than half of trafficked people in the United States are female, and some estimates are as high as 80 percent. Fifty percent of trafficked people are children. While the U.S. government has passed legislation such as the Victims of Trafficking and Violence Protection Act of 2000, human trafficking remains a massive industry in the United States that is "hidden in plain sight," a phrase often used by both government officials and advocates to describe the fact that it is all around us all the time.

Of course, trafficking of persons for labor is not only an international dynamic; trafficking within the United States is also a large-scale problem.

Traffickers target vulnerable populations, such as runaway youths, and, of course, recent immigrants. While in my research I did not directly observe such practices, traffickers are known come into immigration facilities posing as friends or religious workers and recruit people, offering to pay their bonds and give them jobs when they are released. They prey on immigrant shelters like the one Estrella was staying in. Recent immigrants can be highly vulnerable whether or not they are detained, as we saw in Estrella's story. Those in detention may be desperate to get out, and see this as a reasonable option. Those who are not detained need jobs and may not have the knowledge of the cultural context or the language ability necessary to judge whether the offer being made to them is a risky proposition. This may be particularly the case for Indigenous women coming from rural villages and with limited Spanish ability. They are, as Brennan writes, "entering new, unfamiliar labor markets in new, unfamiliar countries and may not be knowledgeable about their basic rights. Their undocumented status . . . ensure[s] that they will remain quiet about abuses. They may not have any place to turn, or fear doing so" (2014:7).

Losing their freedom to traffickers is yet another form of violence Indigenous women migrants may face, and their vulnerability to it is increased by their race, class, gender, and immigration status. Estrella, a young Maya Mam woman clearly suffering from emotional distress, with limited Spanish ability, without a work permit, terrified of being returned to detention or to Guatemala, and living in a migrant shelter, was profoundly vulnerable. Like the other forms of violence women may face from family members, gangs, cartels, government officials, and state policies and practices, trafficking is a facet of market logics of supply and demand that are unfettered by rules or law, and it serves as a venue for yet another group of abusers operating with inexcusable levels of impunity.

The United States bears responsibility here, and not just in the production of labor markets that have a voracious and endless need for exploitable labor, though this is crucial. De Genova (2002) argued long ago that the "illegality" in "illegal" immigration (and thus deportability as well) is the product of immigration laws. Menjívar and Abrego also argue that "migrant illegality (and legality) is legally constructed. . . . Immigration laws restrict the movement of some individuals but allow the admission of others . . . thereby making and unmaking documented, undocumented . . . and quasi-documented immigrants" (2012:1383). These laws are linked directly to particular forms of state subject making that generate a vulnerable and thus exploitable labor population.[11] I have considered U.S. immigration laws and policy because they constitute a significant structural component of the production of Indigenous women migrants' vulnerability. Laws prohibiting labor exploitation through trafficking will continue to make limited headway, because immigration laws are designed to construct vulnerable subjects, ripe for exploitation.

Sanctuary

Hilaria spent months in a small, cramped room at Posada Esperanza, grateful for the shelter but struggling to share the small room with her son Elan and another woman with her two small children as Hilaria and Elan awaited the outcome of Elan's case. Seven months later, on Christmas, she was advised that Elan's asylum was denied and she was informed that they were now deportable. Terrified that they would quickly come for her and Elan, and unwilling to return to Guatemala, Hilaria sought help in the immigrant advocacy community. The following month, she went into sanctuary in a nearby church. She and Elan would spend the next year inside the church as a political campaign was waged by immigration advocates and faith-based activists to gain deferred action status[12] for the two. Though the people in the church were kind, she was sad to find that they were again locked in. A new attorney, this time from a San Antonio–based advocacy organization, took over Elan's case and filed an appeal. In a short-lived victory, in October 2016 Hilaria and Elan were granted deferred action status and prepared to leave the church, poised to start a new life after spending much of the preceding three years in some form of confinement. In November, Donald Trump was elected.

Following the election of Donald Trump, with its accompanying vitriolic and xenophobic rhetoric against immigrants of all kinds, but particularly Latin American and Muslim immigrants, the United States experienced a surge of sanctuary activity. College campuses,[13] cities and municipalities,[14] and even whole states[15] declared themselves sanctuaries for imperiled immigrants. However, the Austin Sanctuary Movement was well into its revival before the Trump era dawned, when immigrants like Hilaria and Elan were already fighting for their safety against policies of refugee deterrence through deportation (see figure 4).

The Sanctuary Movement of the 1980s and early 1990s was a faith-based movement of religious congregations that offered sanctuary to Central Amer-

FIGURE 4 A button supporting Hilaria's campaign for deferred action status on the counter of a local café. Photo by author.

ican refugees fleeing political repression (Coutin 1991; Davidson 1988; Garcia 2018; Golden and McConnell 1986; Tomsho 1987). Though many faced possible torture and death or disappearance in their home countries, the United States' political approach of denying asylum to people fleeing countries which the United States considers to be allies meant that Central Americans were almost universally unsuccessful in obtaining legal asylum status in the United States, with the exception of cases in certain geographic areas. As the Central American wars of the 1980s waned, so too did the Sanctuary Movement. However, many people involved in the original movement continued immigrant advocacy into the 2000s in movements such as No More Deaths/No Mas Muertes, an interfaith coalition founded in 2005 that maintains way stations for immigrants in the Sonoran Desert of Arizona in the context of policies like Operation Gatekeeper in San Diego and Operation Hold-the-Line in El Paso that increasingly channel immigrants through the Sonoran Desert, resulting in increased deaths. Like the Sanctuary Movement, No More Deaths engages not in "civil disobedience" (which suggests violation of the law) but rather in "civil initiative," defined as the right and responsibility of civilians to protect the victims of human rights abuses (Caminero-Santangelo 2009).

Similarly, activists from the earlier Sanctuary Movement played a role in the formation of local detention visitation programs as the numbers of detained immigrants began to rise dramatically in the mid-2000s. In Austin and the surrounding areas, activists involved in the successful campaign and lawsuit that ended family detention in the T. Don Hutto facility, particularly Grassroots Leadership and its suborganization, Texans United for Families, formed the Hutto Visitation Project to provide accompaniment to the women in the now women-only facility and to monitor ongoing conditions inside. After successfully getting this program under way, Grassroots Leadership began helping to build other visitation projects throughout Texas. In 2009 Community Initiatives for Visiting Immigrants in Confinement formed a national network of visitation programs, which grew, by its own account, from the 100 or so activists visiting in four detention centers nationwide to more than 1,400 visiting in forty-three facilities.[16] The Lutheran Immigration and Refugee Service also manage a national network.[17]

The New National Sanctuary Movement is generally understood to have coalesced in Arizona in 2014. Southside Presbyterian Church in Tucson and Shadow Rock United Church of Christ of the Phoenix area, both with roots in the original Sanctuary Movement, were catalysts, harboring a Mexican refugee and a Guatemalan refugee, respectively, and attaining deferred action status for both. Over the next two years, larger numbers of refugees from Mexico and Central America began to arrive, family detention was reinitiated, and extended detention and expedited deportations increased, and local sanctuary movements and networks began to emerge around the country to defend against the detention and deportation of refugees. The Austin Sanctuary Network was formed in 2015 as activists long involved in the Hutto Visitation Project, Grassroots Leadership, Texans United for Families, and the Austin Immigrant Rights Coalition joined forces with area congregations to provide safe refuge and support for asylum seekers who had escaped dangerous and deadly conditions in their countries of origin and who did not want to be deported into those same conditions. In 2015 a queer Guatemalan woman was given sanctuary at the First Unitarian Universalist Church of Austin and won a stay of deportation after a two-and-a-half-month campaign. Hilaria and Elan were the second to seek sanctuary, this time offered by Saint Andrew's Presbyterian Church of Austin. They won a one-year deferred action after an eight-month sanctuary campaign.

The Austin Sanctuary Network has continued to grow, particularly since the election of Donald Trump occuring just after Hilaria's stay of deportation, bringing increased apprehensions and feared deportations.[18] The network now includes clergy who are Presbyterian, Methodist, United Universalist, Seventh-Day Adventist, Baptist, and Episcopal, as well as faith-based organizations such as Jewish Voice for Peace Austin and Bend the Arc.[19] Its mission statement reads, "Our values include honor and respect for every individual and an inclusive community composed of equals with a foundation of non-violence. We confront violent structures and actions with bold compassion and courageous love, standing up for people's rights, regardless of status."[20]

Without a doubt, the Sanctuary Movement offers both a potential refuge and a channel for women to engage in resistance to the latest violences being wrought on them by the U.S. immigration system. Avenues for resistance have been few for women who are geographically dispersed by their release from detention and generally busy trying to survive. In a broader sense, taking sanctuary serves as a contestation of state subject-making, as the "deportable" subject refuses to be constructed as such. It takes tremendous courage (as well as a strong network of people) to undertake such contestation from a position of multiple vulnerability, and the two refugee women in Austin—one queer and one Indigenous, with all the vulnerabilities those subject positions entail—together with dozens around the country who have engaged in this refusal, have made important strides not only in putting the state on notice that they will not accept its state of deportability but also in raising public awareness of the "violent structures and actions" that violate people's rights every day in the United States.

Nevertheless, Hilaria's victory was short-lived. Her concerns about Donald Trump's election proved to be well-founded. Their deferred action status, a product of prosecutorial discretion, would normally have been renewed annually unless their situation in some way had changed. But Donald Trump quickly signaled a conservative stance on discretionary reprieves from removal, ending the Deferred Action for Childhood Arrivals (DACA) program and other country-based deferred action programs. While public advocacy campaigns helped Hilaria to gain a couple of extensions on her deferred action status, eventually ICE declined to renew and ordered her and Elan to appear at the ICE Field Office. Certain they would be taken into custody and deported, Hilaria and Elan did not go to the appointment, but legal and church advocates attended on their behalf. ICE issued deportation orders against them. Hilaria and Elan continue to live in Saint Andrews Church, with the ever-present threat of deportation hanging over their heads.

IN THIS CHAPTER, I have considered the experience of Indigenous women migrants after leaving immigration detention. Not surprisingly, there are a wide range of experiences, though a unifying feature is the wealth of continuing structural impediments to their ability to get free of vulnerability to violence. And, as we saw in relation to domestic violence, the challenging journey north, and immigration detention itself, Indigenous women are particularly subject to these structural barriers because of their race, gender, class, and immigration status.

Also, as we have seen in preceding chapters, the state plays a significant role in shaping this structural vulnerability. In particular, I have examined the ways that U.S. immigration policies and laws constitute legal violence, creating the overarching structure of vulnerability by rendering people deportable, whether practically (by deporting them), or subjectively, by making them continuously subject to potential deportation, and thus subject to separation from loved ones, further violence, or even death in the places that they fled. These laws and policies generate a fear of deportation that, in turn, renders them multiply vulnerable in new ways after their detention. Virgilia is clear that she can never return to the United States without fear of being deported anew. Digna is clear that if deported, she may well be murdered, just as her partner, Marlon, was. Hilaria, even with a stay of deportation in hand, is too apprehensive about her deportability to leave the safety of the church that shelters her and her son.

As I have argued, the race and gender ideologies that play a role in rendering women vulnerable in this context are settler-generated ideologies that have remained permanent features of the structure of the settler state and, in various permutations, continue the same work of controlling and managing populations that pose a perceived risk to settler-state power. Following detention, that control and management is achieved in part through deportation and the production of deportability. Thus, just as mass incarceration constitutes settler elimination, so too does deportation, by literally removing nonwhite others from the landscape and generating conditions of vulnerability that serve the work of controlling and managing populations that pose a risk to settler-state power. Of course, through the vulnerability generated by deportability, the state is facilitating the needs of capitalism, generating a readily exploitable labor base for the voracious markets and drive for profit that characterize neoliberalism. The neoliberal multicriminal settler state thus uses deportability to enable capitalist exploitation (including through illegal markets) and to perpetuate settler control. In this context, as the stories in this chapter demonstrate, Indigenous women migrants are once again multiply *vulneradas*.

Conclusion

Neoliberal Multicriminalism and the Enduring Settler State

The evening news broadcast captured the horror: small children, ripped from their parents' arms and cast into tent cities along the border, or spread throughout the country in various prisonlike facilities. The children did not know where their parents were, or whether they would ever see them again. Their parents suffered the same torture. This broadcast was focused on the reunification of Guatemalan mother Buena Ventura Martin-Godinez with her seven-year-old daughter, Janne (figure 1). I watched from my now entrenched position on the living-room couch, where I had spent countless hours over the year and a half since Trump's election watching the news as the United States, already enmeshed in illegality (I had argued), now descended into open repudiation of any intention to remain a law-abiding state. At the front line of this widespread and open flaunting of domestic and international law were women and children refugees. I stared at the television, battling to subdue the now familiar blend of rage and grief as the heart-wrenching scene unfolded. Janne stands still, arms around her mother's waist, not smiling. She has a glazed look on her face. In the back of my mind, I considered whether one ever recovers from such a trauma, especially one so young. Janne had been in a detention center for sixty-one days. The reporter noted that while thousands of children were separated from their parents during the spring of 2018 based on the Trump administration's "zero tolerance" policy, which explicitly used family separation as a deterrent to further refugee migration, and despite the order of a federal judge in California,[1] such reunifications had been "few and far between." The reporter closed by adding, "This girl does not have Spanish as a first language. She is an indigenous child from Guatemala, which no doubt increased her fear and isolation" (CNN News, July 1, 2018). Angrily brushing aside my tears, I growled uselessly at the television, "Exactly as they intended."

The shattering policy of family separation began after research for this book had ended. Nevertheless, in many senses it represents the culmination of the very processes that I attempted to document. I argued in chapter 1 that in Mexico and Central America, neoliberalism was killing off its multicultural counterpart—hence the term *neoliberal multicriminalism*. While I sought to show how the multicriminalism and ultra-violence of Mexico and Central America were linked to other forms of violence and illegality in the United States through the women's stories, until November 2016 the United States still

FIGURE 5 Buena Ventura Martin-Godinez being reunited with her seven-year-old daughter, Janne. They were separated for sixty-one days. AP Photo/Lynne Sladky.

presented a general commitment to legality that one had to look beyond to recognize the violence. Immigrants, particularly refugee women and children, were the most readily visible crack in the facade of neoliberal multiculturalism in the United States. With Donald Trump's election, the facade would crumble and the U.S. government descend into a disastrous state of illegality.

Nestled among the many heinous acts of the new administration that would defy domestic law, international law, and basic human decency was this gem: in June 2018, Attorney General Jeff Sessions overruled the precedent-setting 2014 case that established domestic violence as a possible ground for asylum.[2] The motivation for this extraordinary ruling was clear, given that it managed to also eliminate refuge for those fleeing gang violence: keeping Central Americans out. Sessions argued in the ruling that asylum claims have expanded too broadly, to include victims of "private violence," such as domestic violence or gang violence.[3] He thus presented an argument that was the opposite of mine: that all forms of violence are interrelated and are very much tied to the state. The real effect of Sessions's act of legal chicanery[4] is that virtually all of the women in this book, and many of the women currently held in immigration prisons throughout the country, will be denied political asylum and will likely be deported. Those arriving will mostly be turned away at the border, without even a chance to have their claims heard. Relegating not just domestic violence but also gang violence to the private sphere allowed the U.S. government to sidestep state accountability and justify the further violence of sending tens of thousands of people back to certain violence and potential death.

Through the course of this book, I have argued, and the women's stories have shown, that the violence they experience is structural in nature and takes place through intersecting axes of oppression that render them multiply vulnerable. By "multiply vulnerable," I do not just mean that they are made vulnerable in different ways at different moments, although they are. I also mean that the multiple axes compound their vulnerability at each moment. In other words, an Indigenous woman migrant is not vulnerable first at home because of her gender, then on the journey because of her race, and then outside her own country because of her immigration status. The intersectional nature of her oppression means that she is profoundly more vulnerable based on all of these at every juncture.

The structural nature of that intersectional oppression implies that the state is not separable from the violence rendered against such women. In chapter 2, we saw how state violence intersected with domestic violence in ways that made understanding domestic violence virtually impossible without taking into account the mutually constituting nature of state racialized and gendered violence, and how these play out through settler-generated ideologies of gender, race, and class. In chapter 3, I argued that the same is true with cartel or gang violence, which might appear distinct from state violence but, as the women's stories showed, in fact is not. The state is intimately involved in this socially organized violence, as a perpetrator and as a generator of the impunity that, in turns, engenders more violence. The race, gender, and class ideologies deployed in this context are calibrated to work with and for neoliberal logics of unbridled market forces, together generating a state of illegality I have characterized as neoliberal multicriminalism. In chapter 4, I examined the ways that the post-9/11 state in the United States constructed immigrants as potential terrorists and criminals, with heavy racial overtones, and then implemented policies and actions that were outside the realm of both domestic and international law, making the U.S. state yet another perpetrator of the violence women experience. Finally, in chapter 5 I analyzed how state deportation and the construction of deportable subjects set the conditions in which new forms of violence can be wrought. Without belaboring the point, we can say that the state is multiply implicated in the myriad forms of violence women suffer. Contrary to Sessions's assertions, there is no private violence.

The state develops its strategies of governance through subject-making in relation to shifting modes of capitalism. As Lisa Lowe powerfully argues in *The Intimacies of Four Continents*, "The social inequalities of our time are a legacy of these processes through which 'the human' is 'freed' by liberal forms, while other subjects, practices, and geographies are placed at a distance from the 'human'" (2015:3). The construction of Indigenous subjects as uncivilized for the purposes of dispossessing them through colonial enclosure, just as African and Asian "arrivants" (Byrd 2011) were constructed as "slaves" and "coolies" in forced-labor systems of enslavement and indenture, takes shape in the current moment in the production of the terrorist or criminal immigrant who must be detained, deported, or deportable. Each of these constructions served a particular moment of capitalist expansion, and each leaves its ideological imprint in racial and gender formations that continue to mark contemporary political subjectivities.

In this book, I have been principally interested in the latest phase of capitalism, neoliberalism, and the ways that its unbridled market logics play out through state policy, criminal activity, and the broad swath of life where the two converge. Early in the book, I suggested that these structuring logics that render women vulnerable are profoundly enduring. While they take different forms, and may seem very different at different times and across distinct geographies, in fact, they are inherent aspects of the settler state generated by European colonial expansion into the rest of the world (though the Americas are of particular interest for my analysis here). Interestingly, the point where the stories presented in this book end, with the election of Donald Trump in November 2016, provides new fodder for this argument.

The election of Trump generated a great deal of consternation in the United States and around the world. Much popular debate took place about whether the president and newly evident swaths of the American public were racist (and misogynist, though this got less attention). Americans, and indeed people throughout the world, seemed surprised that so many people in the United States would vote for a man who believes Mexicans (a stand-in for Latinos) are rapists, Muslims are terrorists, Native Americans are mobsters who fake their ancestry, black people are impoverished inner-city dwellers, and women are pussy to be grabbed (if they are, in his estimation, good-looking enough to qualify for a grab). Analysts scrambled to explain this as "backlash against progress," which, while comforting in the sense that it asserts we haven't spent our whole lives struggling fruitlessly toward rights so tenuous they could vanish overnight, nevertheless is premised on the false notion that there is a unilinear historical progress toward an endpoint variously understood as "postcolonial," "postracial," or "postpatriarchal" society. (The assumptions we hold about this unilinear progress, even as we acknowledge significant back-and-forth, run deep and are exemplified in phrases such as "progressive politics.") Neoliberal multiculturalism had provided an ideological picture of American society that many accepted at face value, allowing them to ignore, or live with, the ongoing oppression of those deemed unqualified in some way for membership and its benefits, or even for survival (see Cacho 2012; Hong 2016; Razack 2015).

The neoliberal multicultural model is in crisis, and the brutal violence of Mexico and Central America amply illustrates the demise of those countries' fledgling multiculturalism. Meanwhile, in recent years the brutal treatment of immigrants—particularly refugee women and children—similarly flagged the decline of the United States' longer-standing multiculturalism, just as police murders of blacks highlighted the fallacy of postracialism. These social dynamics were the canary in the coal mine, signaling that as a justificatory system, multiculturalism was low on oxygen. Trump's election simply brought to the fore contradictions that were already there, and moved the United States along a path not unlike that of Mexico and Central America, in the sense of increased authoritarianism, ruthless pursuit of the welfare of the few over the many, and brutal elimination (through bans, raids, cancellation of status, etc.) of those who are deemed useless or threatening to this project. Not surprisingly, white supremacy, misogyny, and xenophobia have surged.

I have speculated elsewhere that Trump's election and the crash of multiculturalism in many places may in fact signal the beginning of the end of neoliberalism, the contradictions of which are inescapable. Much of Trump's campaign rhetoric was against precisely this globalized neoliberalism (which he associated with the Clintons, though it was his own businesses that had long benefited from the deregulation and outsourcing that globalized neoliberalism implied). Taking up the banner of the white working class, he argued that he would bring the jobs back home, get those pesky immigrants out, and "make America great again." In short, he promised to protect them from the ravages of the neoliberal model and logics that had sacrificed their economic possibilities on the altar of the free market, and ensure that the white settler state remained white. The neoliberal multicultural moment, with its accompanying discourses of tolerance and rights that allowed such notions as a "postracial society" to arise, has reached its limits, and the resurgence of white supremacy and misogyny in public discourse and action is, in one way or another, a direct response to the changing needs of settler-capitalist power.

While it is too early to proclaim the death of neoliberalism—and in any case this book's conclusion is not the place to make the argument—I want to make the point that race, gender, class, and immigration status, always present, are deployed in different ways in different moments in relation to the changing needs of capitalism, and remain key to both enacting and justifying inequality and oppression. In the United States, as in Mexico and Central America—indeed, throughout the modern world since the advent of European colonialism—power has been founded on and structured by the interrelationship of settler colonialism and capitalism, and their attendant logics of race and gender (i.e., white supremacy and patriarchy). While the forms that each of these interrelated structures and logics take over time are historically contingent, they remain as present today as they were five hundred years ago. The error was in believing that the modified "friendlier" forms meant progress toward elimination, rather than new iterations to be recalibrated as the structural needs of power changed. Indeed, we should expect that, long after neoliberalism has faded into some new phase of capitalist exploitation, settler tropes of race, gender, class, and belonging will continue to structure the conditions of possibility for peoples' lives.

Tandayi Achiume has argued that contemporary immigration can be understood as decolonization, in the sense that economic migrants from former European colonies arriving back at the metropole contest—the global structuring of economic inequality that began with the out-migration of at least 62 million people during the nineteenth and early twentieth century (Achiume 2017). This reverse migration, as it were, represents a "rebalancing of the beneficiaries of an asymmetrical system initiated by many of the very same state sovereigns that now self-righteously seek the exclusion of these migrants" (Achiume 2017:143). The women in this book were not principally economic migrants, nor were they arriving to a European metropole of the former colonial power of their countries. However, their migration similarly throws into relief the unsustainable nature of the brutal inequalities generated by the latest phase of settler capitalism—what I call neoliberal multicriminalism—a phrase that made their countries into killing grounds (and has arguably brought the species to the brink of extinction). Achiume's framing of contemporary immigration issues as a direct result of European colonialism and state sovereignty making is refreshing. What a settler frame adds to the analysis is the ability to gauge how states that are a product of that colonial expansion, such as the settler states of the Americas, are fundamentally structured to perpetuate and justify inequality both transnationally and within their own borders. Indeed, settler sovereignty is premised on the state's ability to exclude certain subjects from the benefits of capitalist predations and settler dispossession. While it is difficult to understand the painful journeys of the women portrayed in this book as decolonization, in Achiume's broad envisioning, they can be understood as efforts to rebalance, or at least escape the effects of the most egregious forms of inequality generated by neoliberal multicriminalism—their premature death by violence.

> Marleny lived through several years of abuse as her relationship went downhill. Finally, when her husband began to abuse her daughter, she told him she wanted a divorce. "I didn't want that for my daughter," she said. "I come from a violent family, and the only thing I want is for her to have a fair chance in life [vida justa]." Her husband filed for divorce, claiming adultery and child abuse. He sought full custody of their child. Marleny wasn't letting that happen a second time. She got a lawyer. She tracked down his ex-wife from a previous marriage, and she brought her to court to testify to his abusiveness. He walked in smiling and confident, but Marleny had come prepared. In the end, the judge chastised him for making unsubstantiated claims against her and granted Marleny a divorce, full custody, child support, and a two-year restraining order. Marleny relocated so he couldn't find her, and for the last few years she has been living a life free of interpersonal violence. She works hard cleaning houses and hopes to send her daughter to college so she can live a different kind of life.

It has been my goal to understand how neoliberal settler power works by rendering certain subjects—Indigenous women migrants—multiply vulnerable. The women in this book, beacons of strength and survival, brave their way forward through layer after layer of neoliberal multicriminal violence. As we have seen, they are marked for racialized and gendered state violence, symbolic violence, and physical violence in a myriad of ways at home and on the journey. They show tremendous agency in confronting those assaults on their humanity, only to have their human rights violated yet again throughout detention and postdetention in the United States. In the course of this project, those with legitimate concerns about the dangers of portraying these women as victims have often asked me whether the women are organizing to resist the violence they are subject to. Of course, in specific contexts, the women have organized — notably when they launched the hunger strikes in the detention centers to protest conditions and prolonged incarceration, or sought sanctuary to fight deportation. But my response is no — often they are not organizing to resist the overall matrix of power that generates the multiple violences they experience. These women are not at a place where the kind of social movement organizing that we like to celebrate is an option; they are trying to survive. However, this does not mean they are without agency. What the stories of Indigenous women migrants make evident, above all else, is their strength and resilience as they seek to free themselves of the oppression and violence that mark their lives. More than just agency, I view it as *survivance*, Gerald Vizenor's term for *survival + resistance*. Vizenor famously wrote, "Native survivance stories are renunciations of dominance, tragedy, and victimry" (1999:vii). The women's migration is resistance. By getting out of bed each day, by bravely putting one foot in front of the other and moving forward, by telling their stories, by surviving, they are resisting.

I began this book with Ysinia's story, and it seems fitting to end it with her as well. Ysinia's parting words to me the last time I saw her before her release were, "I hope the next time you come, I will not be here. I will see you again, but this time as a bird set free from its cage." Ysinia, like the other women whose stories are shared here, is no longer incarcerated in the immigrant prisons of Central Texas. She continues, as do the other women portrayed here, in spite of the multiple ways they are *vulneradas*, to work toward a space of freedom for herself even within the structures of power that cage her.

Acknowledgments

The journey of this book was eight years long and was often a rocky path for me. As with any undertaking of such duration, particularly a difficult one, there are many people to thank. First, foremost, I extend my gratitude and respect to the women who shared their stories with me. I am continually humbled by their strength and bravery, and the wisdom their incarcerated stories bring to us.

I am profoundly grateful to have been able to collaborate with the incredible activists and advocates of Grassroots Leadership, the Hutto Visitation Project, and the larger community of immigrant advocates in Austin. Bob Libal, executive director of Grassroots Leadership, works tirelessly toward a world without immigrant incarceration. In the midst of furious organizing around family separation, Bob took time to read the manuscript and give me valuable feedback. Others at Grassroots Leadership also supported and helped the project over the years: thanks for all you do in support of immigrants, Bethany Carson, Sofia Casini, Claudia Muñoz, and Cristina Parker. Rocio Villalobos, who directed the Hutto Visitation Project most of the time I was involved in it, is another fearless warrior-advocate for immigrants. This project would never have advanced from the idea stage without her support and collaboration. Elaine Cohen, who also ran the Hutto Visitation Project and indefatigably visited and supported the women inside the Hutto facility, has been a friend and greatly valued interlocutor throughout. Denise Gilman and Barbara Hines of the Immigration Clinic at the University of Texas Law School do incredible legal work challenging the national security state's injustices. Virginia Raymond, fierce friend and fiercer advocate, is simply a force of nature, as a scholar, as an attorney, as a profoundly human human being. I came to the Hutto Visitation Project through the work of the Social Justice Institute at the University of Texas at Austin, then directed by Eric Tang. I learned much from his ethical position on community-based research, and his solidarity and friendship through some troubling institutional times were invaluable to me.

Though we place our names on them as individuals, all academic works are the product of dialogic engagement. I thank my fellow academics, who working on immigration detention when I was shared their work and their analyses with me generously, especially Lauren Martin, Alicia Re Cruz, and Arantxa Robles.

I was fortunate to benefit from a Mellon Sawyer Seminar grant for "Territorial Roots and Diasporic Routes: Native American and Indigenous Cultural Politics in the Americas" (held with Charles Hale and organized with Luis Carcamo Huechante). The seminar series and all of the participants in it were formative to my thinking on Indigenous diaspora. I also enjoyed institutional support during the research in the form of Faculty Summer Research Grants and a Faculty Research Leave through the Lozano Long Institute of Latin American Studies at UT Austin.

I had many incredible colleagues while I was at UT Austin. Among those who influenced this book directly are (in alphabetical order) Hector Domínguez-Ruvalcaba, Alfonso Gonzalez, Charlie Hale, Juliet Hooker, Luis Carcamo Huechante, Gabriela Polit, Christen Smith, and Rebecca Torres. Among those who made UT an incredible intellectual space, and with whom I variously shared ideas, personal struggles, and university battles (in addition to those colleagues list earlier), were Arturo Arias, Josianna Arroyo, Joao Costa Vargas, Nora England, Karen Engle, Ginnie Garrard, Sue Heinzelman, Lorraine Leu, Kelly McDonough, Martha Menchaca, Jill Robbins, Loriene Roy, Bjorn Sletto, Polly Strong, Circe Sturm, Dustin Tahmahkera, and Luis Urrieta. I hold a special place for Ted Gordon, friend and colleague, who taught me by example how to ethically navigate the dangerous waters of higher-ed administration. Have an exit strategy!

Two-thirds of the way through the writing of this book, I moved from UT Austin to the University of California, Los Angeles. This was a huge move, and leaving the community in Austin behind was very difficult. Fortunately, I stepped into an absolutely incredible group of scholars and activists at UCLA, who quickly became friends as well as colleagues. Leisy Abrego, Can Aciksoz, Hannah Appel, Maylei Blackwell, Jessica Cattelino, Erin Debenport, Mishuana Goeman, Grace Hong, Zenep Korkman, Kelly Lytle Hernández, Purnima Mankekar, Beth Marchant, Terri McCarty, Jemima Pierre, Sherene Razack, Angela Riley, Gaspar Rivera Salgado, and Wendy Teeter, you all inspire me with your brilliant minds and generous hearts.

Having arrived at UCLA, I was extraordinarily fortunate to be able to count on the support of some incredible staff. At the American Indian Studies Center, Clementine Bordeaux, Jamie Chan, Judy De Tar, Pamela Greiman, Stephen Pilcher, Nora Pulskamp, Ken Wade, and Renee White Eyes made my position as director easy. Jamie and Pamela deserve special praise: without them keeping the center rolling smoothly along, I would not have been able to take the final writing time needed to complete this book. I am also grateful for the amazing staff of Gender Studies, masters of taming the beast of public university bureaucracy: Van Do-Nguyen, Samantha Hogan, Richard Medrano, and Jenna Miller-Von Ah. I also much appreciate the staff in my other home, Anthropology: Myrna Dee Castillo Kikvchi, Monica Diaz, Tyler Lawrence, ArmiAnn Manas, Ann Marlons, and Kate Royce. I have had incredibly supportive chairs in Nancy Levine, Beth Marchant, and Jason Throop.

Though it is rare to see higher administrators thanked in acknowledgments, I have been extraordinarily fortunate at UCLA to work under scholars of color who have been tremendously supportive: David Yoo, vice provost for the Institute of American Cultures, and before him, the inimitable Belinda Tucker; and Dean of Social Sciences Darnell Hunt, and before him Interim Dean Laura Gomez. I am so thankful for their support of all my endeavors.

Over the course of the last ten-plus years, I have had the incredible luxury and benefit of working in dialogue with a group of badass women scholars who are studying Indigenous women, legal pluralism, and violence in Mexico, in Guatemala, and at the U.S. border: Aida Hernandez Castillo; Morna Macleod; Mariana Mora; Rachel Seider; Teresa Sierra; Lynn Stephen; Margo Tamez; and Irma Alicia Velasquez Nimatuj, all fierce women, wonderful friends, and gifted scholars. We have come together every couple of years, and our conversations have invariably catapulted my thinking forward. This book would not be the same without those shared conversations. In 2017 we were fortunate to benefit from an exploratory seminar at the Radcliffe Institute for Advanced Study at Harvard University. This meeting—and the input of discussants Kimberley Theidon and John Wilshire Carrera—was critical to my thinking on key issues in the book. I gratefully acknowledge this support.

I am truly appreciative of the readers at the University of North Carolina Press, one anonymous, one named: Marielena Garcia. One could not possibly have asked for better readers, especially for a project such as this. They both understood what I was trying to do, were incredibly supportive, and provided suggestions that were right on and benefited the manuscript immensely.

I also had the great good fortune to benefit from a Research Excellence/Manuscript Workshop held by the Center for the Study of Women at UCLA. What an incredible luxury to have this group of amazing women scholars all read the entire draft manuscript and give me feedback! Leisy Abrego, Maylei Blackwell, Jessica Cattelino, Mishuana Goeman, Grace Hong, Kelly Lytle Hernández, Sherene Razack, and honored guest Lynn Stephen. Much gratitude and love to all of you—you made this book so much better. Special thanks to Maylei for nominating me and facilitating the meeting, and to Grace for organizing it and taking such detailed notes. I gratefully acknowledge the support of the Center for the Study of Women through this terrific program.

In addition to the eight incredible colleagues and two spectacular press readers, several friends also generously read some or all of the draft manuscript and gave me their comments: Marcos Aguilar, Minnie Ferguson, Bob Libal, and Terri McCarty. The book is stronger for their interventions. I appreciate you all so much.

I must also thank the lifelong friends who supported me through this journey. I am grateful to Becky for the gifts of lifelong friendship and short-term concentration. She knows what I mean. Thanks to Woman and King for periodically bringing love and laughter to our house, and to Alisa for being there throughout. Renee and Giuseppe watched me labor over earlier versions in Austin and our shared home, Sombrero Moon. We miss you guys! Kathy Dill, the other half of "gloom and doom" since graduate school, is always there when I need her. Jennifer Bickham Mendez and Angela Stuesse always provide intellectual inspiration, feminist activist solidarity, and unwavering friendship.

The most important acknowledgments go to my family, because without them this book would never have come to completion. My daughter, Camila, has spent a third of her life with me in this project, even riding occasionally to the detention center with me and doing homework in the car while I visited. As the book grew, she grew to adulthood and became the intelligent, funny, beautiful young woman that she is. I am profoundly grateful for the gift that she has given me every day of her life—the experience of a mother's love for her daughter. Love you, baby girl.

No words can convey the gratitude I feel for the love of my life, Joe Berra. This project began the year we married. I am certain I would not have been able to complete it without his seemingly boundless love and support, which allow me to enter the world each day from a place of peace, joy, and wonder. Many of the ideas in this book were forged in dialogues with Joe, an expert on Central America and one of the brightest and most empathic intellects I have ever encountered. Not a day goes by that I do not marvel at my incredible good fortune in having him in my life. I love you, Joe, with all my heart.

Joe brought Josue and Moses into my life, and I could not have asked for more wonderful stepchildren. Thank you for making me part of your family. Camila brought Noah into our family, and I so appreciate his charming, gregarious nature and even-keeled approach to life, as well as his surprising penchant for quirky, high-end fashion. Thanks to Heather for sharing him with us. Returning to Los Angeles brought me closer to my siblings, Kathie, Jamie, Lindsay, Jason, and Christie. Love you all!

My family isn't complete without Chica, Aria, Luna, and Coco. At least 90 percent of this book was written with the three-pound chihuahua Chica on my lap, chocolate pom Aria at my feet, and black panther Luna sitting stealthily nearby. Coco burst on the scene late and has provided significant entertainment value at the end, as only kittens can do. They bring so much love to our lives.

This book is dedicated to my mother, Iris Speed. Her difficult journey toward the end of this life has also coincided with this book's journey. I am grateful for the honor of caring for her, and the privilege of still having her with us. Even from within the cruel ravages of dementia, she continues to teach me about life.

Notes

Chapter One

1. The names of all women migrants throughout the book are pseudonyms. In the redacted versions of their stories, I have slightly altered some identifying details when necessary to protect the identity of the women involved, though I have endeavored to do so without changing the practical facts of the stories or their significance. The oral histories were all gathered between 2012 and 2015 in Austin, Texas, and Chiapas, Mexico, with the exception of one, which was gathered in 2017. Another was updated in follow-up phone conversations in 2018. All conversations took place in Spanish, and the translations to English throughout the book are mine.

2. In *The End of History and the Last Man*, Fukuyama argued that the spread of Western liberal democracy represented not just "the passing of a particular period of postwar history, but the end of history as such: that is, the end point of mankind's ideological evolution and the universalization of Western liberal democracy as the final form of human government" (Fukuyama 1989:4). His work also signaled the triumph of capitalism over communism as the high point of social evolution (in contrast to Marx's arguments) (Fukuyama 1992).

3. See also more recent works on the United States and Canada: Byrd (2011), Coulthard (2014), Simpson (2014).

4. The breakdown by country is as follows: Out of a total of 303,916 apprehensions, 127,938 were from Mexico (42.1 percent); 65,871 from Guatemala (21.6 percent); 49,760 from El Salvador (16.3 percent); and 47,260 from Honduras (15.5 percent). These countries ranked first, second, third, and fourth, respectively, in apprehension numbers. By comparison, India ranked fifth, with only 2,943 apprehensions (U.S. Customs and Border Protection 2017).

5. I use the terms *incarceration* and *immigration prisons* to refer to immigration detention intentionally in order to signal that immigration detention is incarceration and detention facilities are effectively (and often practically) prisons.

6. For a sharp critique of the anthropological nostalgia for, and reification of, "the field," see Berry et al. (2017).

7. Here I make reference to Kelly Lytle Hernández's (2017) brilliant analysis of the rise of human caging in Los Angeles, which is applicable much more broadly in the United States. This work is discussed further in chapter 4.

8. I make reference here to Anibal Quijano's term *coloniality of power*, through which he theorized the legacy of colonialism in contemporary (Latin American) societies, in particular the racialized hierarchical social orders imposed by European colonialism that systematically attribute value to certain peoples and justify the oppression and subordination of others (Quijano 2000). By using *coloniality of anthropology*,

I intend to signal anthropology's key function in regard to that system. This is not a wholesale endorsement of Quijano's work. For an excellent critique from an Indigenous standpoint, see Rivera Cusicanqui (2012). For a gender critique, see Lugones (2007).

9. This is, of course, a generalization. Some excellent work has been done in recent years that seeks to address the politics of knowledge production through activist research. The following is by no means a comprehensive list, but rather a few outstanding examples: Cook (2008), Hale (2006), Kirsh (2006; 2017), Lassiter (2005), Perry (2013), Stephen (2013b), Stuesse (2016) and contributions to the following volumes: Hale (2008) and Sanford and Angel-Ajani (2006).

10. I would note (lest Vine Deloria, Jr. haunt me) that this is a very different undertaking from applied anthropology, designed by anthropologists to "help" Indian people.

11. For readers in fields that do not engage directly with humans as research subjects, the institutional review board human subjects review is a required ethics review that is designed to limit the harms that have been generated in the past by biomedical and social science research on human populations.

12. Notable are the debates around the story of Nobel Peace Prize laureate Rigoberta Menchú in the testimonio work I, *Rigoberta Menchú: An Indian Woman in Guatemala* (Burgos 1983). In 1999 anthropologist David Stoll wrote a book asserting that much of her story was not true. The controversy gave rise to extensive debates about truth, power, history, and the politics of memory (see Arias 2001; 2018).

13. On what I feel to be an offensively regular basis, I am asked whether I should not be taking into account the possibility that the women are all just fabricating their stories in order to gain political asylum in the United States. I have been asked this even by people who are notably progressive or radical in their politics on other issues. My short answer is no. The longer answer that follows, usually only in my head, is that I am frankly astounded at the mental lengths people are willing to go to in order not to have to confront the appalling and intolerable levels of violence that Indigenous women are subject to. If the details of a woman's story shift, or its chronology is off, I see it as a result not of deception but rather of one or more of the following: trauma (well known to cause memory elisions and blocks), cultural difference (particularly notable in relation to narrative and chronology), and fear and anxiety (Are people understanding my poor Spanish? How can I tell/retell this story so that people will understand that my life is at stake?).

14. For example, in a history that is told in chapter 5, a woman named Virgilia recounts how a man who offered her and other immigrants shelter for the night threatened to rape her. I asked Virgilia about the incident, and how he had threatened her. She replied, "I don't remember. Maybe he didn't say anything. I just knew that he would." That Virgilia both experienced it as a rape threat and remembers it as one, in the absence of concrete verbal or physical evidence of a threat, is a product of her positionality as an Indigenous woman, vulnerable to such violence because of her race and gender. What I take from this is not that her story is faulty but that race and gender fundamentally structure the way Indigenous women experience the world, and oral histories may present one unique way of understanding this.

15. In the #MeToo moment, in which certain women's stories have been told and focused on in the national media in the United States, the disjunction of race and gender contributes to the ongoing occlusion of the voices of marginalized women of color such as Indigenous migrants.

16. Saïd Sayrafiezadeh, "How to Write about Trauma," *New York Times Sunday Review*, August 14, 2016, 10.

17. De Genova argued regarding research on undocumented populations, "It is necessary to distinguish between studying undocumented people, on the one hand, and studying 'illegality' and deportability, on the other. The familiar pitfalls by which ethnographic objectification becomes a kind of anthropological pornography—showing it just to show it, as it were—become infinitely more complicated here by the danger that ethnographic disclosure can quite literally become a kind of surveillance, effectively complicit with if not altogether in the service of the state" (2002:422). This risk was also a concern for me in this study, and I have tried, as De Genova's analysis suggests, to depart from the women's experiences to study the dynamics of "vulnerability" and their structural formations, rather than studying the women themselves.

18. In addition, they enter the intense realm of contestation over Indigeneity in the United States, between recognized and nonrecognized tribes, and, in the view of some, constitute another competitor for scarce resources when attempting to claim Indigenous status. This is particularly notable in Southern California, where there are many numerically small tribes that do not enjoy federal recognition, and Indigenous Latin American migrants and their descendants are so numerous that they now make up the largest Indigenous group in the state. It is also a contentious terrain in Texas, where many unrecognized groups are historically transborder and have been denied federal recognition based on the premise that they are Mexican American by descent, as if this precluded their Indigeneity.

19. Indeed, a reflection of this, or perhaps a partial cause of it, is the fact that there is not an available literal translation to the Spanish or a logical linguistic construction for differentiating these forms of colonialism. *Settler* is usually translated into Spanish as *colonizador* or *colono*, which are closer in meaning to "colonizer" or "colonist." At any rate, *colonialismo colonizador* seems preposterously redundant and sheds little light on the distinction the term signals from other forms of colonialism. Perhaps the least confusing term would be *colonialism poblador*. Interestingly, the Google Translate website gives the following example of its usage: "Los españoles fueron los primeros pobladores de muchas regiones de América" (The Spaniards were the first settlers of many regions of America). Nevertheless, in common usage, *poblador* leans much more toward "one who lives in a place" than toward "settler," so I settle for the less-than-ideal *colonialismo de colonos* and note that it is interesting that in Latin, America *settler* and *colonizer* are, at least in linguistic terms, the same thing.

20. McCaa writes that while much about the demographics of Mesoamerica over the centuries is debated, "there is consensus that the sixteenth century was a demographic disaster for Mesoamericans. . . . Estimates of the magnitude of the disaster range from less than twenty-five percent to more than ninety" (2000:242).

21. Before the mid-seventeenth century, the Viceroyalty of New Spain encompassed the Bay Islands, the Cayman Islands, Cuba, Hispañola, Jamaica, Puerto Rico,

Central America to Costa Rica's southern border, Mexico, Florida, all of the southwestern United States (including all or parts of the modern-day U.S. states of California, Nevada, Utah, Colorado, Wyoming, Arizona, New Mexico, Texas, and Florida), and the Mariana Islands and the Philippines.

22. In Mexico, *reducciones* were sometimes called *congregaciones* or *misiones*.

23. Literally, people from the Iberian Peninsula, Spanish-born migrants to the Americas.

24. American-born descendants of Peninsulares.

25. Originally annexed to the Mexican Empire at independence in 1821, the Republic of Central America separated two years later.

26. My intention is not to set up the United States as a unitary model of the settler state against which to compare other states. As Alyosha Goldstein has cogently argued, "Always already shaped by fluctuating interimperial rivalries and counterclaims against the peoples it subsumes, U.S. colonialism has been neither monolithic nor static" (2014:1–2). Yet, as Goldstein goes on to state, "[in the United States] colonialism persists as a never fully repressed or entirely manifest structure, especially as settlers aspire to extinguish Indigenous peoples and variously affirm and naturalize their own status as native to America" (2014:3). This is also true of Mexico and Central America.

27. To be clear, this is not a critique of Native American and Indigenous Studies Association or its council, on which I have served. In fact, as a professional association, it was founded on principles of reaching across geographic and disciplinary divides of the type I am critiquing, and it has done more to move the discipline of Native and Indigenous studies toward hemispheric and global dialogues than any other collective entity in recent memory. I raise the interchange only as evidence (admittedly anecdotal) of the lack of recognition of neoliberalism as a relevant category of study in much of the U.S.-based Native studies field.

28. For example, a recent report by Global Witness (2015) found that that at least 116 environmental activists were murdered in 2014, almost double the number of journalists killed in the same period. Forty percent of those killed were Indigenous, with most people dying amid disputes over hydropower, mining, and agribusiness. Nearly three-quarters of the deaths the report identified were in Central and South America.

Chapter Two

1. I am not entirely comfortable with surviving Indigenous people being referred to as "remnants," but presumably Veracini meant this from the perspective of the logic of the managing state.

2. Castro and Picq relate the specific case of San Pedro de Sacatepéquez, in which on October 13, 1876, Legislative Decree 165 declared that the Maya peoples of the town were from then on ladinos, a measure intended, according to the decree, "to improve the conditions of the Indigenous classes." The decree had one single article declaring that "for legal purposes, the Indians of both sexes in town are declared ladi-

nos, and they will start using the ladino dress by next year" (Castro and Picq 2017:795).

3. This was not unlike the goal of the Indian Office/Bureau of Indian Affairs in the U.S. settler state.

4. Hale goes on to argue that this dichotomy was inverted after the armed conflict ended, with the state embracing some Indigenous rights and ladino elites favoring disciplinary assimilation.

5. Velasquez Nimatuj served as an expert witness in a notable case in which fifteen women from the community of Sepur Zarco, department of Izabal, took retired colonel Estelmer Reyes Girón and former military commissioner Heriberto Asij to trial, both charged with crimes against humanity. Velasquez Nimatuj describes the events: "From 1982 to 1988 the military set up a camp in Sepur Zarco at the orders of landowning families who wanted to take control of the land that the [Indigenous] community was trying to legalize. Soon after their arrival, the security forces murdered the husbands of 15 women who were then raped and forced into sexual and domestic servitude for six years" (2016:5). Velasquez Nimatuj describes the trial: "During the trial, the 15 Q'eqchi' women sat in open court with their faces covered. The stigma of sexual violence was still too much to bear. . . . Hours and hours of [testimony] in which between cries, the women talked about the horrific way in which the army violated them while destroying their family structure and overall way of life. Such was the violence that even the translators had a hard time translating these testimonies. In spite of the pain, with their presence and their voice, these women spoke for the thousands of women who have remained silent or who have died without obtaining justice for the crimes committed against their bodies, minds, families and all community" (2016:5). Most days, during the testimony, members of the Association of Military Veterans of Guatemala stood outside the courthouse and, through a loudspeaker, accused the Q'eqchi' women of being prostitutes. The defense lawyer, in his closing statement, argued that because of their condition of poverty, the Indigenous women had resorted to prostitution in the military barracks, and thus, no crime was committed against them. This case set a precedent nationwide because the courts accepted sexual violence as a weapon of war in the Guatemalan context and, internationally, this was the first time that the trial took place in the country where the abuses occurred.

6. In 1925, also a period of national consolidation following the social turbulence of the Mexican Revolution, José Vasconcelos, a philosopher who also served as the secretary of education from 1921 to 1924 and later would be a presidential candidate (1929), published the book *La raza cósmica*, in which he argued that "Iberoamericans" constituted a "fifth race" made up of a blend of the "four races."

7. I have written about this more extensively in Speed (2007), but during prior research conducted over the course of a decade in Mexico, I regularly had people tell me that they "used to be Indigenous" before they moved to the city, lost their language, or stopped wearing traditional clothes. I worked with the community of Nicolas Ruiz, which filed a complaint against the Mexican government before the International Labour Organization based on Convention 169 on Indigenous and Tribal

Peoples, charging that their rights were violated by the government's refusal to recognize them as an Indigenous pueblo because they no longer spoke Tzeltal.

Chapter Three

1. Some people use the term *pollero* and some the term *coyote* to refer to traffickers. While some people argue that *pollero* is the specific individual who brings one across the border and *coyote* can refer to traffickers more generally (who may be involved in other aspects of the smuggling business), in my experience people used them interchangeably. I have respected the language each woman used, and the terms should be considered interchangeable here.

2. Marleny is the only woman represented in this book who is not Indigenous. While Indigenous identity did not play a role in what happened to her, it is worth noting that Central Americans are racialized and discriminated against in Mexico in ways that invoke discourses about Indigenousness, including references to brown skin and lower-class status. Derogatory terms like *cachuco* (roughly, "dirty pig") capture this sentiment (see Vogt 2016).

3. Tracy Wilkinson, "In Honduras, Rival Gangs Keep a Death Grip on San Pedro Sula," *Los Angeles Times*, December 17, 2013, http://www.latimes.com/world/la-fg-c1-honduras-violence-20131216-dto-htmlstory.html.

4. The leader of the coup, Honduran general Romeo Vásquez Velásquez, and others, such as General Luis Javier Prince Suazo, who played an important role in the coup as head of the Honduran Air Force, were trained at the School of the Americas, a U.S. Army training program notorious for the number of graduates who have engaged in coups, as well as the torture and murder of political opponents. Stephen Zunes, "The U.S. Role in the Honduras Coup and Subsequent Violence," *Huffington Post*, June 19, 2016, http://www.huffingtonpost.com/entry/the-us-role-in-the-honduras-coup-and-subsequent-violence_us_5766c7ebe4b0092652d7a138.

5. Mark Weisbrot, "Hard Choices: Hillary Clinton Admits Role in Honduran Coup Aftermath," *Al-Jazeera*, September 29, 2014, http://america.aljazeera.com/opinions/2014/9/hillary-clinton-honduraslatinamericaforeignpolicy.html.

6. Wilkinson, "In Honduras."

7. Note the emblematic case of Bertha Cáceras, a Lenca environmental rights activist and founder and coordinator of the Council of Popular and Indigenous Organizations of Honduras, who won major international awards for her activism and opposition to dams and other extractivist projects. She was murdered in her home in La Esperanza, Honduras, on March 3, 2016, in an extrajudicial killing planned by military intelligence specialists linked to the country's U.S.-trained Special Forces. For more on the Special Forces connection, see Nina Lahkani, "Berta Cáceres Court Papers Show Murder Suspects' Links to US-Trained Elite Troops," *Guardian*, February 28, 2017, https://www.theguardian.com/world/2017/feb/28/berta-caceres-honduras-military-intelligence-us-trained-special-forces.

8. I lost touch with Nadania before being able to fully capture her story. There are a number of women I met whose stories do not appear in the book. However, I should

emphasize that nothing in those stories contradicted the analysis presented here. In other words, I did not choose to use only stories that supported my argument.

9. Don Batteletti, "Reynosa, Mexico: Where the Cartels Rule," *Los Angeles Times*, November 5, 2010, http://framework.latimes.com/2010/11/05/reynosa-mexico-where -the-cartels-rule/#/0.

10. "Mexico Migrants Face Human Rights Crisis, Says Amnesty," *BBC News*, April 28, 2010, http://news.bbc.co.uk/2/hi/8647252.stm. In the same report, the National Human Rights Commission estimated that in one six-month period during 2009, the families of immigrants paid at least $25 million in ransom to kidnappers (Casillas 2011).

11. Silvia Otero, "Juez Dicta arresto contra cuatro generales por narco," *El Universal*, August 1, 2012, http://www.eluniversal.com.mx/nacion/198877.html.

12. The five-member Grupo Interdisciplinario de Expertos Independientes (GIEI) was appointed by Comisión Interamericana de Derechos Humanos, a body of the Organization of American States.

13. Wilkinson, "6 Hidden Mass Graves May Hold Missing Mexican Students," *Los Angeles Times*, October 5, 2014, http://www.latimes.com/world/mexico-americas/la -fg-hidden-graves-mexico-missing-students-20141005-story.html. Marcela Turati, "Durante Busqueda de normalistas han sido hallados 55 cadáveres y 50 fosas," *Proceso*, December 3, 2014, https://www.proceso.com.mx/389708/durante-busqueda -de-normalistas-han-sido-hallados-55-cadaveres-y-50-fosas.

14. See, for example, "Mexico: 59 Bodies Found in Mass Grave," *Telegraph*, April 7, 2001, http://www.telegraph.co.uk/news/worldnews/centralamericaandthecaribbean /mexico/8433955/Mexico-59-bodies-found-in-mass-grave.html; and Associated Press, "Argentine Team Excavates Migrant Graves in Mexico," *San Diego Union-Tribune*, August 21, 2012, https://www.sandiegouniontribune.com/sdut-argentine-team-excavates -migrant-graves-in-mexico-2012aug21-story.html, regarding more than eighty bodies excavated from graves in Chiapas.

15. "Murdered Bodies Found in Mexico Were Migrants," *BBC News*, August 25, 2010, http://www.bbc.co.uk/news/world-latin-america-11090563.

16. Tuckerman, "Mexican Drug Cartel Massacres Have Method in Their Brutal Madness," *Guardian*, May 14, 2012, http://www.guardian.co.uk/world/2012/may /14/mexico-drug-cartel-massacres-analysis?newsfeed=true.

17. Linthicum, "Mexico's Bloody Drug War Is Killing More People than Ever," *Los Angeles Times*, July 22, 2017, http://www.latimes.com/world/mexico-americas/la-fg -mexico-murders-20170721-story.html.

18. Persio, "Crime in Mexico: Murder Rate Reached Record High and Nobody Is Talking about It," *Newsweek*, June 22, 2017, http://www.newsweek.com/crime -mexico-murder-rate-reaches-record-high-and-nobody-talking-about-it-628193.

19. Reported in Persio.

20. "Inside the Opioid Epidemic," *Economist*, May 11, 2017, https://www.economist .com/news/united-states/21721960-deaths-drugs-say-more-about-markets-about -white-despair-inside-opioid; "America's Opioid Epidemic Is Worsening," *Economist*, March 6, 2017, https://www.economist.com/blogs/graphicdetail/2017/03/daily-chart-3; "US Heroin Use Has Increased Almost Fivefold in a Decade, Study Shows," *Guardian*,

March 29, 2017, https://www.theguardian.com/society/2017/mar/29/us-heroin-use
-has-increased-almost-fivefold-in-a-decade-study-shows.

21. Chapo Guzman stood trial in Brooklyn, New York, from November 2018 to February 2019. He was convicted on all counts. The trial involved extensive testimony detailing gruesome violence and massive corruption at every level of the Mexican government.

Chapter Four

1. The Customs and Border Protection short-term holding facilities are popularly referred to as "iceboxes" because they are maintained at such low temperatures. Detained people are given Mylar blankets, which they often interpret as aluminum paper, and often are packed into the iceboxes in very overcrowded conditions.

2. Casillas (2011:299) also references a series of other acts affecting immigrants and reflecting the shift toward interpellating immigrants as terrorists: the Enhanced Border Security and Visa Entry Reform Act (2002); the National Security Entry-Exit Registration System (2002); the U.S. Visitor and Immigrant Status Indicator Technology program (2003); the Student and Exchange Visitor Information System (2003); the Security and Prosperity Partnership of North America (March 2005) in Canada, the United States, and Mexico; the Operation against Smugglers (and Traffickers) Initiative on Safety and Security (August 2005), a bilateral Mexico-U.S. program to find and prosecute smugglers of undocumented immigrants; and the U.S. Secure Borders Initiative (November 2005).

3. See Preston, "Huge Amounts Spent on Immigration, Study Finds," *New York Times*, January 7, 2013.

4. Ted Robbins, "Little-Known Immigration Mandate Keeps Detention Beds Full," *NPR*, November 19, 2013, https://www.npr.org/2013/11/19/245968601/little-known
-immigration-mandate-keeps-detention-beds-full.

5. ThinkProgress reports that in 2014, CCA made $195,022,000, while GEO made $143,840,000 in profits. Esther Yu His, "Millions Spent Lobbying By Private Prison Corporations To Keep A Quota Of Arrested Immigrants, Report Says," ThinkProgress, April 16, 2015, https://thinkprogress.org/millions-spent-lobbying-by-private
-prison-corporations-to-keep-a-quota-of-arrested-immigrants-report-c68e82916819/.

6. If women detained by Customs and Border Protection express fear of returning to their country, they should be flagged for a credible fear assessment by an asylum officer. If this happens (and it doesn't always, as will be discussed further in chapter 5), they are sent to a detention facility and soon meet, often via video call, with an asylum officer from U.S. Citizenship and Immigration Services who determines whether their fear of return is "credible"—that is, whether there is a significant possibility that they will prevail in immigration court in their claim for asylum or protection from deportation to a country where they are likely to face violence or death. This step is hugely significant because if they are deemed not to have a credible fear, they are placed in expedited removal and remain in detention until they are deported. Many women understand this simply as having lost their case, though in fact they never reached the stage of having a case.

7. "ACLU Challenges Prison-Like Conditions at Hutto Detention Center," ACLU, March 6, 2007, https://www.aclu.org/immigrants-rights-racial-justice-prisoners -rights/aclu-challenges-prison-conditions-hutto-detention.

8. Flores v. Meese Agreement, ACLU, August 12, 1996, https://www.aclu.org/files /pdfs/immigrants/flores_v_meese_agreement.pdf.

9. Bernstein, "U.S. to Reform Policy on Detention for Immigrants," *New York Times*, August 5, 2009, http://www.nytimes.com/2009/08/06/us/politics/06detain.html ?mcubz=3.

10. "Landmark Settlement Announced in Federal Lawsuit Challenging Conditions in Immigrant Detention Center in Texas," ACLU, August 27, 2007, https://www.aclu .org/news/landmark-settlement-announced-federal-lawsuit-challenging -conditions-immigrant-detention-center.

11. Cocian, "CCA Guard Accused of 8 Sexual Assaults," Courthouse News Service, April 15, 2015, https://www.courthousenews.com/cca-guard-accused-of-8-sexual -assaults/.

12. "Sexual Abuse of Female Detainees at Hutto Highlights Ongoing Failure of Im- migration Detention System, Says ACLU," ACLU, August 20, 2010, https://www .aclu.org/news/sexual-abuse-female-detainees-hutto-highlights-ongoing-failure -immigration-detention-system.

13. Seville, "Sex Abuse Alleged at Immigrant Family Detention Center in Texas," NBC News, October 2, 2014, http://www.nbcnews.com/storyline/immigration -border-crisis/sex-abuse-alleged-immigrant-family-detention-center-texas -n217166.

14. Preston, "Report Finds No Evidence of Abuse at Immigration Center in Texas," *New York Times*, February 6, 2015, https://www.nytimes.com/2015/02/07/us/report -finds-no-evidence-of-sexual-abuse-at-texas-immigration-detention-center.html.

15. John Roth, Inspector General, Office of the Inspector General, Department of Homeland Security, to Honorable Jeh C. Johnson, Secretary of Homeland Security, memorandum, January 7, 2015, https://www.oig.dhs.gov/assets/Mga/OIG_mga-010715 .pdf.

16. Roth to Johnson.

17. Ortiz, "At Congressional Forum, Social Worker and Formerly-Detained Moms Testify about Horrific Conditions at Karnes," *America's Voice* (blog), July 29, 2015, http://americasvoice.org/blog/at-congressional-forum-social-worker-and-formerly -detained-moms-testify-about-horrific-conditions-at-karnes/.

18. Hennessey-Fiske, "Ex-Worker at Karnes Immigrant Detention Center Says She Saw Unethical Behavior," *Los Angeles Times*, July 27, 2015, http://www.latimes .com/nation/la-na-olivia-lopez-karnes-detention-center-20150727-story.html.

19. Hennessey-Fiske.

20. "South Texas ICE Detention Facility to House Adults with Children," Depart- ment of Homeland Security, July 31, 2014, https://www.dhs.gov/news/2014/07/31 /south-texas-ice-detention-facility-house-adults-children.

21. ICE bond hearing documentation packet, in possession of the author.

22. R. I. L-R, et al., Plaintiffs, v. Jeh Charles Johnson, et al., Defendants, Civil Ac- tion No. 15-11 (JEB) (D.D.C. 2015) (memorandum opinion), 34.

23. Palkington, "'Soul-Destroying': One Woman's Story of Life at Dilley Detention Center," *Guardian*, May 22, 2015, https://www.theguardian.com/us-news/2015/may/22/immigrant-mothers-dilley-family-detention-center-texas.

24. Breisblatt, "Texas Judge Rules Immigration Family Detention Centers Cannot Get Childcare Licenses," American Immigration Council, December 6, 2016, http://immigrationimpact.com/2016/12/06/texas-judge-rules-immigration-family-detention-centers-cannot-get-childcare-licenses/.

25. Breisblatt.

26. "Court Rules That Family Detention Violates Flores Agreement," Human Rights First, June 28, 2017, http://www.humanrightsfirst.org/press-release/court-rules-family-detention-violates-flores-agreement.

27. Zaya, "Declaration" (unpublished manuscript in possession of the author, 2015), 5.

28. Zaya, 5–6.

29. Orduñez, "Exclusive: Family Detention Social Worker Speaks Out," McClatchy DC Bureau, July 27, 2015, http://www.mcclatchydc.com/news/nation-world/national/article28696174.html.

30. Kassie, "Sexual Assault inside Detention: Two Survivors Tell Their Stories," *New York Times*, July 17, 2018, https://www.nytimes.com/2018/07/17/us/sexual-assault-ice-detention-survivor-stories.html.

31. "Sexual Assault in Immigration Detention," Community Initiatives for Visiting Immigrants in Confinement, April 11, 2017, http://www.endisolation.org/sexual-assault-in-immigration-detention/.

32. Elisa Foley, "Prison Rape Elimination Act to Expand to Immigrant Detention Centers," *Huffington Post*, May 17, 2012, http://www.huffingtonpost.com/2012/05/17/prison-rape-elimination-act-immigrant-detention_n_1524470.html; "DOJ PREA Regulations Encouraging but Fail to Protect Immigration Detainees," ACLU, May 17, 2012, https://www.aclu.org/news/doj-prea-regulations-encouraging-fail-protect-immigration-detainees.

33. Kanjobal, K'iche, Kachiquel, and Mam are the most commonly spoken Mayan languages in the United States, and they are the ones in which the Border Patrol provides printed materials. Other Mayan languages (there are twenty-two spoken in Guatemala alone) are less likely to be available.

34. The CARA Family Detention Pro Bono Project is a partnership of four organizations: the Catholic Legal Immigration Network, the American Immigration Lawyers Association, the Refugee and Immigrant Center for Education and Legal Services, and the American Immigration Council.

35. CARA Family Detention Pro Bono Project to Megan Mack, Office of Civil Rights and Civil Liberties, Department of Homeland Security, and John Roth, Office of Inspector General, Department of Homeland Security, "Re: Family Detention—Challenges Faced by Indigenous Language Speakers," letter of complaint, December 10, 2015, http://www.aila.org/advo-media/press-releases/2015/crcl-complaint-challenges-faced-family-detention.

36. See U.S. Government Accountability Office 2010:32, 40, 41, cited in CARA Family Detention Pro Bono Project to Mack and Roth.

37. CARA Family Detention Pro Bono Project to Mack and Roth.

38. See chapter 1, note 18.

39. Quoted by permission of the author.

Chapter Five

1. Marchevsky and Baker, "Why Has President Obama Deported More Immigrants than Any President in US History?," *The Nation*, March 31, 2014, https://www.thenation.com/article/why-has-president-obama-deported-more-immigrants-any-president-us-history/.

2. Young, "The Hard Truths about Obama's Deportation Priorities," *Huffington Post*, February 27, 2017, http://www.huffingtonpost.com/entry/hard-truths-about-obamas-deportation-priorities_us_58b3c9e7e4b0658fc20f979e.

3. Thompson and Flagg, "Who Is ICE Deporting? Obama's Promise to Focus on 'Felons Not Families' Has Fallen Short," Marshall Project, September 26, 2016, https://www.themarshallproject.org/2016/09/26/who-is-ice-deporting#.EqwJk50Nr.

4. Marchevsky and Baker, "Why Has President Obama?"

5. In fact, "fast-tracking" was the logical extension of policies long in place. In the mid-1990s Heyman described the "voluntary-departure complex," in which "deportable aliens" apprehended at the U.S.-Mexico border (at that time, overwhelmingly Mexican) "are permitted (indeed, encouraged) to waive their rights to a deportation hearing and return to Mexico without lengthy detention, expensive bonding, and trial" (1995:266–67; see discussion in Di Genova 2002). Migrants returned to Mexico in this way were free to try again (and possibly get caught and try again until they succeed), creating a rotating door that raises apprehension numbers for the government and generates the impression of border control while still allowing a cheap labor flow into the United States. This practice has also been informally referred to as "catch and release."

6. Brodzinsky and Pilkington, "US Government Deporting Central American Migrants to Their Deaths," *Guardian*, October 12, 2015, https://www.theguardian.com/us-news/2015/oct/12/obama-immigration-deportations-central-america.

7. Kilpatrick, "Into the Arms of the Cartels: Deported Mexicans Sent to Cities Ruled by Fear," *Al Jazeera*, October 16, 2014.

8. Marchevsky and Baker, "Why Has President Obama?"

9. They may have a master calendar hearing pending to set the date of their merits hearing, or, if they change venue, they will have one or more master calendar hearings to set the final date for the merits hearing (where their case will be adjudicated).

10. While the official Secure Communities program was ended in 2014 with the Priority Enforcement program (felons, not families), collaboration among local law enforcement continues.

11. Writing about the pre-ICE era, De Genova argues, "There has never been sufficient funding for the INS to evacuate the United States of undocumented migrants by means of deportations, nor even for the Border Patrol to 'hold the line.' The INS is neither equipped nor intended to actually keep the undocumented out. The very existence of the enforcement branches of the INS (and the Border Patrol, in particular) is

premised upon the continued presence of migrants whose undocumented legal status has long been equated with the disposable (deportable), ultimately 'temporary' character of the commodity that is their labor-power" (2002:438).

12. *Deferred action* means that ICE/DHS has agreed temporarily to refrain from acting on the deportation order against them. That deferred action can be revoked at any time, though it is generally renewed barring change of circumstances.

13. "Sanctuary Campuses," Google Maps, accessed December 7, 2018, https://www .google.com/maps/d/viewer?mid=1LcIME474-lYWbTf_xQChIhSSN30&hl=en&ll =36.20397974434345%2C-113.89148150000005&z=3.

14. Rathod, "Here Are the Sanctuary Cities Ready to Resist Trump's Deportation Threats," *Mother Jones*, December 2, 2016, http://www.motherjones.com/politics /2016/12/sanctuary-city-immigration-federal-deportation-trump-threats-budget/.

15. Steinmetz, "California Senate Passes 'Sanctuary State' Bill," *Time*, April 3, 2017, http://time.com/4724121/california-sanctuary-state-bill-passes-senate-immigration/.

16. Freedom for Immigrants (formerly Community Initiatives for Visiting Immigrants in Confinement) website, accessed May 2017, http://www.endisolation.org /about/our-innovation/.

17. Lutheran Immigration and Refugee Service website, accessed May 2017, https://www.lirs.org/.

18. Numbers released by the DHS in August 2017 showed that, in fact, in the first six months of the Trump administration, apprehensions of immigrants had increased, while deportations had decreased from the levels of the Obama administration. In the last three months of the Obama administration, ICE averaged 9,134 arrests per month. Under Trump, that number has increased each month, averaging 13,085 a month between February and June. However, in those same months, ICE averaged 22,705 deportations per month under Obama, and averaged 16,895 under Trump. Bendix, "Immigrant Arrests Are Up, but Deportation Is Down," *Atlantic*, May 17, 2017, https://www.theatlantic.com/news/archive/2017/05/under-trump-immigrants -arrests-are-up-but-deportation-is-down/527103/.

19. Personal communication with Elaine Cohen, Austin Sanctuary Network founder and activist. September 7, 2017.

20. https://austinsanctuarynetwork.org/.

Conclusion

1. Jarrett, "Federal Judge Orders Reunification of Parents and Children, End to Most Family Separations at Border," CNN, June 27, 2018, https://www.cnn.com/2018 /06/26/politics/federal-court-order-family-separations/index.html.

2. Stern, "Jeff Sessions' Latest Immigration Ruling Is a Violation of International Law: An Interview with Archi Pyati about the Dire Consequences of Matter of A-B-," *Slate*, June 14, 2018, https://slate.com/news-and-politics/2018/06/jeff-sessions-ruling -in-matter-of-a-b-is-a-violation-of-international-law.html.

3. Matter of A-B-, 27 I&N Dec. 316 (A.G. 2018), https://www.justice.gov/eoir/page /file/1070866/download. For a news article explaining the impact, see Benner and Dickerson, "Sessions Says Domestic and Gang Violence Are Not Grounds for Asylum,"

New York Times, June 11, 2018, https://www.nytimes.com/2018/06/11/us/politics/sessions -domestic-violence-asylum.html.

4. Bischoff, "Jeff Sessions Is Hijacking Immigration Law: How the Attorney General Is Abusing a Rarely Used Provision to Rewrite Legal Precedent," *Slate*, June 13, 2018, https://slate.com/news-and-politics/2018/06/in-matter-of-a-b-jeff-sessions -hijacked-immigration-law-by-abusing-a-rarely-used-provision.html. See also Stern, "Jeff Sessions' Latest Immigration Ruling."

Bibliography

Achiume, Tendaye. 2017. "Reimagining International Law for Global Migration: Immigration as Decolonization?" *American Journal of International Law* 111:142–46.

Ackerman, Alissa R., and Rich Furman. 2013. "The Criminalization of Immigration and the Privatization of the Immigration Detention: Implications for Justice." *Contemporary Justice Review* 16(2): 251–63.

Alexander, Michelle. 2012. *The New Jim Crow: Mass Incarceration in the Age of Colorblindness*. New Press, New York.

American Immigration Lawyers Association. 2015. "The Real Alternatives to Family Detention." July 8, 2015. http://www.aila.org/infonet/the-real-alternatives-to -family-detention.

———. 2016. *Due Process Denied: Central Americans Seeking Asylum and Legal Protection in the United States*. Doc. No. 16061461. American Immigration Lawyers Association, Washington, DC.

Amnesty International. 2008. *Maze of Injustice: The Failure to Protect Indigenous Women from Sexual Violence in the USA*. Amnesty International, New York.

———. 2009. *Jailed without Justice: Immigration Detention in the USA*. Amnesty International, New York. http://www.amnestyusa.org/research/reports/usa -jailed-without-justice.

———. 2010. *Invisible Victims: Migrants on the Move in Mexico*. Amnesty International, London.

———. 2012. "Sexual Abuse in Immigration Detention Facilities." http://www.aclu .org/sexual-abuse-immigration-detention.

Anglin, Mary K. 1998. "Feminist perspectives on structural violence," *Identities* 5:2, 145–51.

Aquino Moreschi, Alejandra. 2009. "Entre el 'sueño zapatista' y el 'sueño americano': La migración a Estados Unidos vista desde las comunidades zapatistas." *Migración y desarrollo* 13:79–95.

———. 2010. "Migrantes chiapanecos en Estados Unidos: Los nuevos nómadas laborales." *Migración Internacional* 5(4): 369–68.

Archibald, Jo-ann. 2008. *Indigenous Storywork: Educating the Heart, Mind, Body, and Spirit*. UBC Press, Vancouver.

Archuleta, Elizabeth. 2006. "'I Give You Back': Indigenous Women Writing to Survive." *Studies in American Indian Literatures* 18(4): 88–114.

Arias, Arturo. 2001. *The Rigoberta Menchú Controversy*. University of Minnesota Press, Minneapolis.

———. 2018. "After the Rigoberta Menchu Controversy: Lessons Learned about the Nature of Subalterity and the Specifics of the Indigenous Subject." *MLA* 117(2): 481–505.

Arias, Enrique, and Daniel Goldstein. 2010. *Violent Pluralism: Understanding the New Democracies of Latin America*. Duke University Press, Durham, NC.

Bachman, Ronet, Heather Zaykowski, Rachel Kallmyer, Margarita Poteyeva, and Christina Lanier. 2008. *Violence against American Indian and Alaska Native Women and the Criminal Justice Response: What Is Known*. Report to the U.S. Department of Justice. https://www.ncjrs.gov/pdffiles1/nij/grants/223691.pdf.

Beck, Allen J., Marcus Berzofsky, Rachel Caspar, and Christopher Krebs. 2012. *Sexual Victimization In Prisons And Jails Reported By Inmates, 2011-12-Update*. Bureau of Justice Statistics. https://www.bjs.gov/index.cfm?ty=pbdetail&iid =4654.

Benson, Peter. 2008. "En el Campo: Faciality and Structural Violence in Migrant Labor Camps." *Cultural Anthropology* 23(4): 589–629.

Berry, Maya J., Claudia Chavez Arguelles, Shanya Cordis, Sarah Ihmoud, and Ruth Elizabeth Velasquez Estrada. 2017. "Toward a Fugitive Anthropology: Gender, Race, and Violence in the Field." *Cultural Anthropology* 32(4): 537–65.

Biolsi, Thomas. 2007. *Deadliest Enemies: Law and Race Relations on and off Rosebud Reservation*. University of Minnesota Press, Minneapolis.

Bird, Gloria. 1997. "Breaking the Silence: Writing as 'Witness.'" In *Speaking for the Generations: Native Writers on Writing*, ed. Simon J. Ortiz, 63–74. University of Arizona Press, Tucson.

Blackwell, Maylei. 2011. *Chicana Power! Contested Histories of Feminism in the Chicana Movement*. University of Texas Press, Austin.

Blackwell, Maylei, Floridalma Boj López, and Luis Urrieta. 2017. "Special Issue: Critical Latinx Indigeneities." *Latino Studies* 15:126–37.

Bourgois, Philippe. 2001. "The Power of Violence in War and Peace: Post-Cold War Lessons from El Salvador." *Ethnography* 2(1): 5–34.

Bourgois, Philippe, and Nancy Scheper Hughes. 2004. "Comment on 'An Anthropology of Structural Violence' by Paul Farmer." *Current Anthropology* 45(3): 317–18.

Brands, Hal. 2015. *Crime, Violence, and the Crisis in Guatemala: A Case Study in the Erosion of the State*. CreateSpace Independent Publishing Platform.

Brant, Beth. 1995. *Writing as Witness: Essay and Talk*. Three O'Clock Press, Toronto.

Brennan, Denise. 2014. *Life Interrupted: Trafficking into Forced Labor in the United States*. Duke University Press, Durham, NC.

Briscoe, Ivan, and Martin Rodríguez Pellecer. 2010. *A State under Siege: Elites, Criminal Networks, and Institutional Reform in Guatemala*. Netherlands Institute of International Relations, The Hague.

Buff, Rachel Ida. 2018. *Against the Deportation Terror: Organizing for Immigrant Rights in the Twentieth Century*. Temple University Press, Philadelphia.

Burgos, Elizabeth. 1983. *I, Rigoberta Menchú: An Indian Woman in Guatemala*. Verso, New York.

Burrell, Jennifer L. 2005. "Migration and the Transnationalization of Fiesta Customs in Todos Santos Cuchumatán, Guatemala." *Latin American Perspectives* 32(5): 12–32.

Butler, Judith, Zenep Gambetti, and Leticia Sabsay, eds. 2016. *Vulnerability in Resistance*. Duke University Press, Durham, NC.

Byrd, Jodi. 2011. *The Transit of Empire: Indigenous Critiques of Colonialism*. University of Minnesota Press, Minneapolis.

Cacho, Lisa Marie. 2012. *Social Death: Racialized Rightlessness and the Criminalization of the Unprotected*. New York University Press, New York.

Caminero-Santangelo, Marta. 2009. "Responding to the Human Costs of US Immigration Policy: No More Deaths and the New Sanctuary Movement." *Latino Studies* 7(1): 112–22.

Campbell, Howard. 2009. *Drug War Zone: Frontline Dispatches from the Streets of El Paso and Juarez*. University of Texas Press, Austin.

———. 2011. "No end in sight: violence in Ciudad Juárez." *NACLA Report on the Americas* (May/June): 19–22.

———. 2012. "Narco-Propaganda in the Mexican 'Drug War': An Anthropological Perspective." *Latin American Perspectives* 41:60–77.

Canada National Clearinghouse on Family Violence. 2008. *Aboriginal Women and Family Violence*. Public Health Agency of Canada, Ottawa.

Carson, Bethany, and Eleana Diaz. 2015. *Payoff: How Congress Ensures Private Prison Profit with an Immigrant Detention Quota*. Grassroots Leadership, Austin, TX.

Casaus Arzú, Marta. 1995. *Guatemala: Linaje y racismo*. Facultad Latinoamericana de Ciencias Sociales. San Jose, Costa Rica.

Casillas, Rodolfo. 2011. "The Dark Side of Globalized Migration: The Rise and Peak of Criminal Networks: The Case of Central Americans in Mexico." *Globalizations* 8(3): 295–310.

Castellanos, Bianet. 2017. "Introduction: Settler Colonialism in Latin America." *American Quarterly* 69(4): 777–81.

Castro, Juan, and Manuela Lavinas Picq. 2017. "Stateness as Landgrab: A Political History of Maya Dispossession in Guatemala." *American Quarterly* 69(4): 791–99.

Cockburn, Cynthia. 2004. "The Continuum of Violence: A Gender Perspective on War and Peace." In *Sites of Violence: Gender and Conflict Zones*, ed. Wenona Giles and Jennifer Hyndman, 22–44. University of California Press, Berkeley.

Collins, Jane L., Micaela di Leonardo, and Brett Williams, eds. 2008. *New Landscapes of Inequality: Neoliberalism and the Erosion of Democracy in America*. School for Advanced Research, Santa Fe.

Collins, Patricia Hill. 1998. "The Tie That Binds: Race, Gender, and US Violence." *Ethnic and Racial Studies* 21(5): 917–38.

Comision Nacional de Derechos Humanos. 2011. *Informe Especial sobre secuestro de migrantes en México*. CNDH, Mexico City.

Comisión Nacional para el Desarrollo de los Pueblos Indígenas. 2016. "Datos e indicadores sobre violencia contra las mujeres indígenas." https://www.gob.mx /inpi/articulos/datos-e-indicadores-sobre-violencia-contra-las-mujeres -indigenas.

Commission for Historical Clarification. 1999. *Guatemala: Memory of Silence*. https://www.documentcloud.org/documents/357870-guatemala-memory-of -silence-the-commission-for.html.

Cook, Samuel R. 2008. "'You Can't Put a Price on It': Activist Anthropology in the Mountaintop Removal Debate." *Collaborative Anthropologies* 1:138–62.

Cornelius, Wayne, David Fitzgerald, and Pedro Lewin Fischer, eds. 2007. *Mayan Journeys: The New Migration from Yucatan to the United States*. Center for Comparative Immigration Studies, University of California, San Diego, La Jolla.

Corrales, Manuel. 2012. "The Future of Mexico's Drug Strategy." Council on Hemispheric Affairs, May 9, 2012. http://www.coha.org/the-future-of-mexicos -drug-strategy/.

Coulthard, Glen. 2014. *Red Skin, White Masks: Rejecting the Colonial Politics of Recognition*. University of Minnesota Press, Minneapolis.

Coutin, Susan Bibler. 1991. "The Culture of Protest: Religious Activism and the U.S. Sanctuary Movement." PhD dissertation, Stanford University.

———. 2005. "Being En Route." *American Anthropologist* 107(2): 195–206.

Craven, Christa, and Dána-Ain Davis, eds. 2013. *Feminist Activist Ethnography: Counterpoints to Neoliberalism in North America*. Lexington Books, Lanham, MD.

Crenshaw, Kimberlé. 1991. "Mapping the Margins: Intersectionality, Identity Politics, and Violence against Women of Color." *Stanford Law Review* 43(6): 1241–99.

———. 2012. "From Private Violence to Mass Incarceration: Thinking Intersectionally about Women, Race, and Social Control." *UCLA Law Review* 59:1418–72.

Crosby, Alison, and M. Brinton Lykes. 2011. "Mayan Women Survivors Speak: The Gendered Relations of Truth Telling in Postwar Guatemala." *International Journal of Transitional Justice* 5:456–76.

Cumes, Aura Estela, and Ana Silvia Monzón, eds. 2006. *La encrucijada de las identidades: Mujeres feminismos y mayanismos*. Intervida World Alliance, Guatemala City.

Das, Veena. 2000. *Violence and Subjectivity*. University of California Press, Berkeley.

———. 2008. "Violence, Gender, and Subjectivity." *Annual Review of Anthropology* 37:283–99.

Das Gupta, Monisha. Forthcoming. "Introduction: Deportation as Settler Carcerality." In *Settling Migration: Migrant Organizing in the Era of Deportation and Dispossession*. Draft chapter manuscript in possession of the author.

Das Gupta, Monisha, and Sue P. Haglund. 2015. "Mexican Migration to Hawai'i and US Settler Colonialism." *Latino Studies* 13:455–80.

Davidson, Miriam. 1988. *Convictions of the Heart: Jim Corbett and the Sanctuary Movement*. University of Arizona Press, Tucson.

Deer, Sarah. 2005. "Toward an Indigenous Jurisprudence of Rape." *Kansas Journal of Law and Public Policy* 14:121–54.

De Genova, Nicolas. 2002. "Migrant 'Illegality' and Deportability in Everyday Life." *Annual Review of Anthropology* 31:419–47.

De Leon, Jason. 2015. *The Land of Open Graves: Living and Dying on the Migrant Trail*. University of California Press, Berkeley.

Deloria, Vine, Jr. 1969. *Custer Died for Your Sins*. Macmillan, New York.

Department of Homeland Security (DHS). 2016. *DHS Immigration Enforcement: 2016*. Annual Flow Report. Department of Homeland Security, Washington, DC. https://www.dhs.gov/immigration-statistics/enforcement-priorities.

Diaz Polanco, Héctor. 1997. *Indigenous Peoples in Latin America: The Quest for Self Determination*. Perseus, New York.

Domínguez Rubalcava, Héctor, and Patricia Ravelo Blancas. 2010. "Obedience without Compliance: The Role of the Government, Organized Crime, and NGOs in the System of Impunity That Murders the Women of Ciudad Juárez." In *Terrorizing Women: Feminicide in the Americas*, ed. Rosa-Linda Fregoso and Cynthia Bejarano, 182–96. Duke University Press, Durham, NC.

Dominguez Villegas, Rodrigo. 2014. "Central American Migrants and 'La Bestia': The Route, Dangers, and Government Responses." Migration Policy Institute, September 10, 2014. http://www.migrationpolicy.org/article/central-american
-migrants-and-%E2%80%9Cla-bestia%E2%80%9D-route-dangers-and-government
-responses.

Eagly, Ingrid, and Steven Shafer. 2016. *Access to Counsel in Immigration Court*. American Immigration Council, Washington, DC.

Equipo de Estudios Comunitaros y Acción Psicosocial and Union Nacional de Mujeres Guatemaltecas. 2011. *Los tejidos que lleva el alma: Memoria de las mujeres mayas sobrevivientes de la violación sexual durante el conflicto armado*. F&G Editors, Guatemala City.

Erez, Edna, Madelaine Adelman, and Carol Gregory. 2009. "Intersections of Immigration and Domestic Violence: Voices of Battered Immigrant Women." *Feminist Criminology* 4(1): 32–56.

Farmer, Paul. 2004. "An Anthropology of Structural Violence." *Current Anthropology* 45(3): 305–25.

Feingold, David A. 2005. "Human Trafficking." *Foreign Policy* 150:26–32.

Feltz, Renee, and Stokely Baksh. 2009. "Business of Detention." In *Beyond Walls and Cages: Prisons, Borders, and Global Crisis*, ed. Jenna M. Loyd, Matt Mitchelson, and Andrew Burridge. University of Georgia Press, Athens, GA.

Fernández-Kelly, Patricia, and Douglas Massey. 2007. "Borders for Whom? The Role of NAFTA in Mexico-U.S. Migration." *Annals of the American Academy of Political and Social Science* 610:98–118.

Ford, Lisa. 2010. *Settler Sovereignty*. Harvard Historical Studies. Harvard University Press, Cambridge, MA.

Fox, Jonathan, and Gaspar Rivera-Salgado. 2004a. "Building Civil Society among Indigenous Migrants." In *Indigenous Mexican Migrants in the United States*, ed. Jonathan Fox and Gaspar Rivera-Salgado, 1–65. Center for U.S.-Mexican Studies and Center for Comparative Immigration Studies, University of California, San Diego, La Jolla.

———, eds. 2004b. *Indígenas mexicanos migrantes en los Estados Unidos*. University of California, Santa Cruz; Universidad de Zacatecas, Mexico; Miguel Ángel Porrúa, Mexico City.

Foxen, Patricia. 2008. *In Search of Providence: Transnational Mayan Identities*. Vanderbilt University Press, Nashville.

Franco, Celinda. 2007. *The MS-13 and 18th Street Gangs: Emerging Transnational Gang Threats?* Congressional Research Service Report for Congress RL34233. https://
www.files.ethz.ch/isn/118413/2007-11-02_Gangs_Threat.pdf.

Fregoso, Rosa-Linda, and Cynthia Bejarano. 2010a. "Introduction: A Cartography of Feminicide in the Americas." In *Terrorizing Women: Feminicide in the Americas*, ed. Rosa-Linda Fregoso and Cynthia Bejarano, 1–42. Duke University Press, Durham, NC.

———, eds. 2010b. *Terrorizing Women: Feminicide in the Americas*. Duke University Press, Durham, NC.

Fukuyama, Francis. 1989. "The End of History." *National Interest* (Summer): 3–18.

———. 1992. *The End of History and the Last Man*. Free Press, New York.

Galtung, Johan. 1969. "Violence, Peace and Peace Research." *Journal of Peace Research* 6(3): 167–91.

Garcia, Mario. 2018. *Father Luis Olivares, a Biography: Faith Politics and the Origins of the Sanctuary Movement in Los Angeles*. University of North Carolina Press, Chapel Hill, NC.

García, María Elena. 2005. *Making Indigenous Citizens: Identities, Education, and Multicultural Development in Peru*. Stanford University Press, Stanford, CA.

García Hernández, César Cuauhtémoc. 2013. "Creating Crimmigration." *Brigham Young University Law Review* 2013(6): 1457–516.

———. 2017. *Crimmigration Law*. American Bar Association, Washington, DC.

Gavigan, Patrick. 2011. "Organized Crime, Illicit Power, and Threatened Peace Process: The Case of Guatemala." In *Peace Operations and Organized Crime: Enemies of Allies?*, ed. Jame Cockayne and Adam Cupel, 99–115. Routledge, New York.

Giles, Wenona, and Jennifer Hyndman. 2004. "Introduction: Gender and Conflict in a Global Context." In *Sites of Violence: Gender and Conflict Zones*, ed. Wenona Giles and Jennifer Hyndman, 3–23. University of California Press, Berkeley.

Gilman, Denise. 2012. "Realizing Liberty: The Use of International Human Rights Law to Realign Detention in the United States." *Fordham International Law Review* 36:244–333.

Gilmore, Ruth. 2007. *Golden Gulag: Prisons, Surplus, Crisis, and Opposition in Globalizing California*. University of California Press, Berkeley, CA.

Giroux, Henry A. 2011. "Neoliberalism and the Death of the Social State: Remembering Walter Benjamin's Angel of History." *Social Identities* 17(4): 587–601.

Gledhill, John. 2005. "Neoliberalism." In *Companion to an Anthropology of Politics*, ed. David Nugent and Joan Vincent, 332–48. Blackwell, New York.

Global Witness. 2015. *How Many More?* Global Witness, London.

Godoy-Paiz, Paula. 2008. "Women in Guatemala's Metropolitan Area: Violence, Law, and Social Justice." *Studies in Social Justice* 2(1): 27–47.

Goeman, Mishuana. 2013. *Mark My Words: Native Women Mapping Out Nations*. University of Minnesota Press, Minneapolis.

Golden, Remmy, and Michael McConnell. 1986. *Sanctuary: The New Underground Railroad*. Orbis Books, Ossining, NY.

Goldstein, Alyosha. 2014. "Introduction: Toward a Genealogy of the U.S. Colonial Present." In *Formations of United States Colonialism*, ed. A. Goldstein. Duke University Press, Durham, NC.

Gomez, Juan, and Manuela Lavinas Picq. 2017. "Stateness as Landgrab: A Political History of Maya Dispossession in Guatemala." *American Quarterly* 61(4): 791–99.

Gonzales, Alfonso. 2013. *Reform without Justice: Latino Migrant Politics and the Homeland Security State*. Oxford University Press, Oxford.

Gordon, Todd, and Jeffery R. Webber. 2013. "Post-coup Honduras: Latin America's Corridor of Reaction." *Historical Materialism* 21(3): 16–56.

Gott, Richard. 2007. "Latin America as White Settler Society." *Bulletin of Latin American Research* 26(2): 271–89.

Gottschalk, Marie. 2008. "Hiding in Plain Sight: American Politics and the Carceral State." *Annual Review of Political Science* 11:235–60.

Grassroots Leadership. 2016. "The Facts about Family Detention." Last updated February 29, 2016. https://grassrootsleadership.org/facts-about-family -detention.

Grayson, George W. 2010. *Mexico: Narco-violence and a Failed State?* Transaction, New Brunswick, NJ.

Grupo Interdisciplinario de Expertos Independientes. 2016. *Informe Ayotzinapa: Investigación y primeras conclusionesde las desapariciones y homicidios de los normalistas de Ayotzinapa*. http://www.oas.org/es/cidh/actividades/giei/GIEI -InformeAyotzinapa1.pdf.

Guia, Maria Joao, Maartje van der Woude, and Joanne van der Leun, eds. 2013. *Social Control and Justice: Crimmigration in the Age of Fear*. Eleven International, The Hague.

Gupta, Akhil. 2012. *Red Tape: Bureaucracy, Structural Violence, and Poverty in India*. Duke University Press, Durham, NC.

Gurney, Kyra. 2014. "Honduras Solves 1% of Homicide Cases: Report." InSight Crime, December 2014. http://www.insightcrime.org/news-briefs/honduras -solves-1-of-homicide-cases.

Gutierrez, Natividad. 1995. "Miscegenation as nation-building: Indian and immigrant women in Mexico." In *Unsettling Settler Societies: Articulations of Gender, Race, Ethnicity and Class*, ed. Daiva Stasiulis and Nira Yuval-Davis, 161–86. Sage, London.

Hale, Charles R. 2002. "Does Multiculturalism Menace? Governance, Cultural Rights and the Politics of Identity in Guatemala." *Journal of Latin American Studies* 34(3): 485–524.

———. 2005. "Neoliberal Multiculturalism: The Remaking of Cultural Rights and Racial Dominance in Central America." *Political and Legal Anthropology Review* 28(1): 10–28.

———. 2006. *Más que un Indio: Racial Ambivalence and Neoliberal Multiculturalism in Guatemala*. School of American Research, Santa Fe.

———, ed. 2008. *Engaging Contradictions: Activist Scholarship in Interdisciplinary Perspective*. University of California Press, Berkeley.

Harvey, David. 2004. "The 'New' Imperialism: Accumulation by Disspossesion." *Socialist Register* 40: 63–87.

———. 2007. "Neoliberalism and the City." *Studies in Social Justice* 1(1): 2–13.

Harvey, Penelope, and Peter Gow, eds. 2013. *Sex and Violence: Issues in Representation*. Routledge, London, and New York.

Hastings, Julie A. 2002. "Silencing State-Sponsored Rape: In and beyond a Transnational Guatemalan Community." *Violence against Women* 8(10): 1153–81.

Hernández, Anabel. 2012. *México en Llamas: El legado de Calderón*. Grijalbo, Mexico City, Mexico.

Hernández, R. Aída, Sarela Paz, and María Teresa Sierra. 2004. *El estado y los indígenas en tiempos del PAN: Neo-indigenismo, legalidad e identidad*. CIESAS, Mexico City, Mexico.

Hernández Castillo, Rosalva Aída, ed. 1998. *La otra palabra: Mujeres y violencia en Chiapas antes y después de Acteal*. Grupo de Mujeres de San Cristóbal, Centro de Investigación y Acción para la Mujer y CIESAS, San Cristobal de Las Casas, Mexico.

Hernández, Rosalva Aída, and Shannon Speed. 2012. "Mujeres indígenas presas en México y Estados Unidos: Un desafío hemisférico para los estudios indígenas." *LASA Forum* 43(1): 17–20.

Heyman, Josiah McC. 1995. "Putting Power in the Anthropology of Bureaucracy: The Immigration and Naturalization Service at the Mexico-United States Border." *Current Anthropology* 36(2): 261–87.

Hine-Ramsberger, William. 2011. "Drug Violence and Constitutional Revisions: Mexico's 2008 Criminal Justice Reform and the Formation of the Rule of Law." *Brooklyn Journal of International Law* 37(1): 292–318.

Hispanic Economics. n.d. "Mexican Native Americans Decline to Cooperate with the US Census." Accessed December 7, 2018. http://www.hispaniceconomics.com /overviewofushispanics/mexicannativeamericans.html.

Holmes, Seth. 2013. *Fresh Fruit, Broken Bodies: Migrant Farmworkers in the United States*. University of California Press, Berkeley.

Homeland Security Act. 2002. Pub. L. No. 107-296, 116 Stat. 2135. https://www.dhs .gov/xabout/laws/law_regulation_rule_0011.shtm.

Hong, Grace Kyungwon. 2016. *Death beyond Disavowal: The Impossible Politics of Difference*. University of Minnesota Press, Minneapolis.

Huhndorf, Shari M., and Cheryl Suzack. 2010. "Indigenous Feminism: Theorizing the Issues." In *Indigenous Women and Feminism: Politics, Activism, Culture*, ed. Cheryl Suzack, Shari M. Huhndorf, Jeanne Perreault, and Jean Barman, 1–17. UBC Press, Vancouver.

Huizar, Javier, and Isidro Cerda. 2004. "Indigenous Mexican Migrants in the 2000 U.S. Census: Hispanic American Indians." In *Indigenous Mexican Migrants in the United States*, ed. Jonathan Fox and Gaspar Rivera-Salgado, 279–302. Center for U.S.-Mexican Studies and Center for Comparative Immigration Studies, University of California, San Diego, La Jolla.

Human Rights Watch. 2010. *Detained and at Risk: Sexual Abuse and Harassment in US Immigration Detention*. Human Rights Watch, New York.

———. 2014a. *US: Migrants Returned to Danger: Serious Flaws in Border Screening of Fleeing Central Americans*. Human Rights Watch, New York.

———. 2014b. *"You Don't Have Rights Here": US Border Screening and Returns of Central Americans to Risk of Serious Harm*. Human Rights Watch, New York.

Humes, Karen, Nicolas Jones, and Roberto Ramírez. 2011. "Overview of Race and Hispanic Origin: 2010." United States Census Bureau. http://www.census.gov /prod/cen2010/briefs/c2010br-02.pdf.

Immigration and Customs Enforcement (ICE). 2012. "Secure Communities." https://www.ice.gov/secure-communities.

Indian Law Resource Center. "Violence Against Native Women Gaining Global Attention." https://indianlaw.org/safewomen/violence-against-native-women-gaining-global-attention.

InSight Crime. 2015. "Special Report: Gangs in Honduras." December 9, 2015. https://www.insightcrime.org/investigations/special-report-gangs-in-honduras/.

Instituto Nacional de Estadistica. 2017. *Estadísticas de Violencia en contra de la Mujer 2014-2016*. Instituto Nacional de Estadistica, Guatemala City.

Jackson, Shona. 2012. *Creole Indigeneity: Between Myth and Nation in the Caribbean*. University of Minnesota Press, Minneapolis.

Jameson, Fredrick. 1992. *Postmodernism, or, The Cultural Logic of Late Capitalism*. Duke University Press, Durham, NC.

Jiménez Váldez, Else Ivette. 2014. "Mujeres, narco y violencia: Resultados de una guerra fallida." *Región y Sociedad*, número especial 4:101–28.

Karaim, Reed. 2015. "Immigrant Detention: Is the System Too Harsh?" *CQ Researcher* 25(38): 889–912.

Kauanui, J. Kēhaulani. 2016. "'A Structure, Not an Event': Settler Colonialism and Enduring Indigeneity." *Lateral* 5(1). http://csalateral.org/wp/issue/5-1/forum-alt-humanities-settler-colonialism-enduring-indigeneity-kauanui/.

Kearny, Michael. 1995. "The Effects of Transnational Culture, Economy, and Migration on Mixtec Identity in Oaxacalifornia." In *The Bubbling Cauldron: Race, Ethnicity, and the Urban Crisis*, ed. Michael P. Smith and Joe R. Feagin, 226–43. University of Minnesota Press, Minneapolis.

Keel, Monique. 2004. *Family Violence and Sexual Assault in Indigenous Communities: "Walking the Talk."* Briefing No. 4. Australian Institute of Family Studies, Melbourne.

Kelly, Liz. 1987. "The Continuum of Sexual Violence." In *Women, Violence and Social Control*, ed. Jalna Hanmer and Mary Maynard, 46–60. Humanities Press International, Atlantic Highlands, NJ.

Kirsch, Stuart. 2006. *Reverse Anthropology: Indigenous Analysis of Social and Environmental Relations in New Guinea*. Stanford University Press, Stanford, CA.

———. 2017. *Engaged Anthropology: Politics Beyond the Text*. University of California Press, Berkeley.

Lassiter, Luke Eric. 2005. *The Chicago Guide to Collaborative Ethnography*. University of Chicago Press, Chicago, IL.

Levinson, Deborah. 2013. *Adiós Niño: The Gangs of Guatemala City and the Politics of Death*. Duke University Press, Durham, NC.

Loperena, Christopher. 2017. "Settler Violence?: Race and Emergent Frontiers of Progress in Honduras." *American Quarterly* 69(4): 801–7.

Lowe, Lisa. 2015. *The Intimacies of Four Continents*. Duke University Press, Durham, NC.

Lugones, Maria. 2007. "Heterosexualism and the Colonial/Modern Gender System." *Hypatia* 22(1): 186–209.

Lytle Hernández, Kelly. 2017. *City of Inmates: Conquest, Rebellion, and the Rise of Human Caging in Los Angeles, 1771–1965*. University of North Carolina Press, Chapel Hill.

MacKenzie, C. James. 2016. *Indigenous Bodies, Maya Minds: Religion and Modernity in a Transnational K'iche' Community*. University of Colorado Press, Boulder.

Maddison, Sarah. 2013. "Indigenous Identity, 'Authenticity' and the Structural Violence of Settler Colonialism." *Identities: Global Studies in Culture and Power* 20(3): 288–303.

Main, Alexander. 2010. "'A New Chapter of Engagement': Obama and the Honduran Coup." *NACLA Report on the Americas* 43(1): 15–21.

Manz, Beatriz. 1988. *Refugees of a Hidden War: The Aftermath of Counterinsurgency in Guatemala*. State University of New York Press, Albany.

Martin, Lauren. 2011. "The Geopolitics of Vulnerability: Children's Legal Subjectivity, Immigrant Family Detention and US Immigration Law and Enforcement Policy." *Gender, Place and Culture* 18(4): 477–98.

———. 2015. "Noncitizen Detention: Spatial Strategies of Migrant Precarity in US Immigration and Border Control." *Annales de géographie* 2(702–3): 231–47.

Martinez, Denis Roberto. 2014. *Youth under the Gun: Violence, Fear, and Resistance in Urban Guatemala*, PhD dissertation, University of Texas at Austin.

Martínez, Oscar. 2010. *Los migrantes que no importan: En el camino con los centroamericanos indocumentados en México*. Colección Cuadernos de crónica, Edición Icaria, Barcelona.

Matthews, Graham, and Sam Goodman, eds. 2013. *Violence and the Limits of Representation*. Palgrave MacMillan, New York.

McCaa, Robert. 2000. "The Peopling of Mexico from Origins to Revolution." In *A Population History of North America*, ed. Michael R. Haines and Richard H. Steckel, 241–304. Cambridge University Press, Cambridge.

McDonald, James H., and John P. Hawkins. 2013. "Introduction: Crisis of Governance and Consequences of Indeterminacy in Postwar Maya Guatemala." In *Crisis of Governance in Maya Guatemala: Indigenous Responses to a Failing State*, ed. John P. Hawkins, James H. McDonald, and Marlon Randolph Adams, 13–49. University of Oklahoma Press, Norman.

Meissner, Doris, Donald L. Kerwin, Muzzafar Chishti, and Claire Bergeron. 2013. *Immigration Enforcement in the United States: The Rise of a Formidable Machinery*. Migration Policy Institute, Washington, DC.

Menjívar, Cecilia. 2012. "Violencia en la vida de las mujeres en Guatemala." In *Diálogos interdisciplinarios sobre violencia sexual*, ed. Patricia Ravelo Blancas and Héctor Domínguez Ruvalcaba, 211–34. FONCA, Mexico City.

Menjívar, Cecilia, and Leisy Abrego. 2012. "Legal Violence: Immigration Law and the Lives of Central American Immigrants." *American Journal of Sociology* 117(5): 1380–421.

Menjívar, Cecilia, and Olivia Salcido. 2002. "Immigrant Women and Domestic Violence: Common Experiences in Different Countries." *Gender and Society* 16(6): 898–920.

Million, Dian. 2009. "Felt Theory: An Indigenous Feminist Approach to Affect and History." *Wicazo Sa Review* 24(2): 53–76.

Mills, James. 1986. *The Underground Empire: Where Crime and Governments Embrace*. Dell, Ney York, NY.

Morgensen, Scott Lauria. 2010. "Settler Homonationalism: Theorizing Settler Colonialism within Queer Modernities." *GLQ: A Journal of Lesbian and Gay Studies* 16(1–2): 105–31.

Moser, Caroline O. N. 2001. "The Gendered Continuum of Violence and Conflict." In *Victims, Perpetrators, or Actors? Gender, Armed Conflict, and Political Violence*, ed. Caroline O. N. Moser and Fiona Clark, 30–51. Zed Books, London.

Moser, Caroline O. N., and Fiona Clark. 2001a. Introduction to *Victims, Perpetrators, or Actors? Gender, Armed Conflict, and Political Violence*, ed. Caroline O. N. Moser and Fiona Clark, 3–12. Zed Books, London.

———, eds. 2001b. *Victims, Perpetrators, or Actors? Gender, Armed Conflict, and Political Violence*. Zed Books, London.

National Prison Rape Elimination Commission. 2009. *National Prison Rape Elimination Commission Report*. http://www.ncjrs.gov/pdffiles1/226680.pdf.

Nazario, Sonia. 2007. *Enrique's Journey*. Random House, New York.

Noferi, Mark. 2015. *A Humane Approach Can Work: The Effectiveness of Alternatives to Detention for Asylum Seekers*. Center for Migration Studies, New York; American Immigration Council, Washington, DC. https://www .americanimmigrationcouncil.org/research/humane-approach-can-work -effectiveness-alternatives-detention-asylum-seekers.

Observatorio Nacional de la Violencia de la Universidad Nacional Autónoma de Honduras. 2018. "Muerte Violenta de Mujeres y Femicidios." https://iudpas.unah .edu.hn/observatorio-de-la-violencia/boletines-del-observatorio-2/unidad-de -genero/.

Office of the Federal Detention Trustee. 2002. *Detention Needs Assessment and Baseline Report: A Compendium of Federal Detention Statistics*. U.S. Department of Justice Office of the Federal Detention Trustee, Washington, DC. https://www.justice .gov/archive/ofdt/compendium_final.pdf.

Office of the United Nations High Commissioner for Human Rights (OHCHR). 2011. "Report to the UN High Commissioner for Human Rights Committee." https:// www2.ohchr.org/english/ohchrreport2011/web_version/ohchr_report2011_web /allegati/downloads/o_Whole_OHCHR_Report_2011.pdf.

Olivera, Mercedes. 2006. "Violencia Feminicida: Violence against Women and Mexico's Structural Crisis." *Latin American Perspectives* 33(2): 104–14.

———. 2010. "Violencia Feminicida: Violence against women and Mexico's Structural Crisis." In *Terrorizing Women: Feminicide in the Americas*, ed. Rosa-Linda Fregoso and Cynthia Bejarano, 49–58. Duke University Press, Durham, NC.

Orren, Karen, and Stephen Skowronek. 2004. *The Search for American Political Development*. Cambridge University Press, Cambridge.

Ortiz, Simon J., ed. 1997. *Speaking for the Generations: Native Writers on Writing*. University of Arizona Press, Tucson.

Ostry, Jonathan D., Prakash Loungani, and Davide Furceri. 2016. "Neoliberalism: Oversold?" *Finance and Development* 53(2): 38–41.

Pachico, Elyssa. 2015. "Latin America Dominates List of World's Most Violent Cities." InSight Crime, January 2015. http://www.insightcrime.org/news-analysis /latin-america-dominates-list-of-worlds-most-violent-cities.

Paley, Dawn. 2014. *Drug War Capitalism*. AK Press, Oakland, CA.

Park, Yun-Joo, and Patricia Richards. 2007. "Negotiating Neoliberal Multiculturalism: Mapuche Workers in the Chilean State." *Social Forces* 85(3): 1319–39.

Pasternak, Shiri. 2014. "Where Do Laws Meet? Jurisdiction and Settler Colonialism." *Canadian Journal of Law and Society / Revue Canadienne Droit et Société* 29(2): 145–61.

Pedraza Fariña, Laura, Spring Miller, and James L. Cavallaro. 2010. *No Place to Hide: Gang, State, and Clandestine Violence in El Salvador*. International Human Rights Program Practice Series. Harvard Law School, Cambridge, MA.

Perry, Keisha-Khan. 2013. *Black Women against the Land Grab: The Fight for Racial Justice in Brazil*. University of Minnesota Press, Minneapolis, MN.

Pine, Adrienne. 2008. *Working Hard, Drinking Hard: On Violence and Survival in Honduras*. University of California Press, Berkeley.

Poppa, Terrence. 2010. *Drug Lord: The Life and Death of a Mexican Kingpin*. Cinco Puntos Press, El Paso.

Postero, Nancy. 2006. *Now We Are Citizens: Indigenous Politics in Postmulticultural Bolivia*. Stanford University Press, Stanford, CA.

Price, Joshua M. 2012. *Structural Violence: Hidden Brutality in the Lives of Women*. State University of New York Press, Albany.

Quijano, Anibal. 2000. "Colonialidad de Poder, Eurocentrismo, y América Latina." In *Colonialidad del saber, eurocentrismo y ciencias sicales*. CLACSO-UNESCO 2000, Buenos Aires, Argentina.

Ray, Anita, and Jay Silverman. 2002. "Violence against Immigrant Women: The Roles of Culture, Context, and Legal Immigrant Status on Intimate Partner Violence." *Violence against Women* 8(3): 367–98.

Razack, Sherene. 2010. "Gendered Racial Violence and Spacialized Justice: The Murder of Pamela George." *Canadian Journal of Law and Society* 15(2): 91–130.

———. 2015. *Dying from Improvement: Inquests and Inquiries into Indigenous Death in Custody*. University of Toronto Press, Toronto.

———. 2016. "Gendering Disposability." *Canadian Journal of Women and Law / Revue Femmes et Droit* 9:285–307.

Reforma Constitucional en Materia de Justicia Penal y Seguridad Pública. Published in the Official Registry of the Federation, Mexico City, June 18, 2008.

Reimann, Allison W. 2009. "Hope for the Future? The Asylum Claims of Women Fleeing Sexual Violence in Guatemala." *University of Pennsylvania Law Review* 157:1199–262.

Reina, Angelica S., Brenda J. Lohman, and Marta María Maldonado. 2014. "'He Said They'd Deport Me': Factors Influencing Domestic Violence Help-Seeking Practices among Latina Immigrants." *Journal of Interpersonal Violence* 29(4): 593–615.

Restall, Matthew, Lisa Sousa, and Kevin Terraciano. 2005. *Mesoamerican Voices: Native Language Writings from Colonial Mexico, Yucatan and Guatemala*. Cambridge University Press, Cambridge.

Riddle, Carrie Cross. 2017. "Structural Violence, Intersectionality, and Justpeace: Evaluating Women's Peacebuilding Agency in Manipur, India." *Hypatia* 32(3): 576–92.

Rivera Cusicanqui, Silvia. 2012. "*Ch'ixinakax utxiwa*: A Reflection on the Practices and Discourses of Decolonization." *South Atlantic Quarterly* 111(1): 95–109.

Rodriguez, Nestor, and Cecilia Menjívar. 2015. "Central American Immigrants and Racialization in a Post–Civil Rights Era." In *How the United States Racializes Latinos: White Hegemony and Its Consequences*, ed. Jose A. Cobas, Jorge Duany, and Joe R. Feagin, 183–99. Routledge, New York.

Rosas, Gilberto. 2012. *Barrio Libre: Criminalizing States and Delinquent Refusals of the New Frontier*. Duke University Press, Durham, NC.

Rosay, André. 2018. "Violence Against American Indian and Alaska Native Women and Men." National Justice Institute. https://nij.gov/journals/277/pages/violence -against-american-indians-alaska-natives.aspx.

Rothstein, Melissa, and Lovisa Stannow. 2009. *Improving Prison Oversight to Address Sexual Violence in Detention*. American Constitution Society for Law and Policy, Washington, DC. https://www.acslaw.org/wp-content/uploads/2018/05 /Rothstein-Stannow-Issue-Brief.pdf.

Rouse, Roger. 1991. "Mexican Migration and the Space of Postmodernism." *Diaspora* 1(1): 8–23.

Saldaña Portillo, María Josefina. 2016. *Indian Given: Racial Geographies across Mexico and the United States*. Duke University Press, Durham, NC.

Sanford, Victoria. 2008. "From Genocide to Feminicide: Impunity and Human Rights in Twenty-First Century Guatemala." *Journal of Human Rights* 7(2): 104–22.

Sanford, Victoria, and Asale Angel-Ajani. 2006. *Engaged Observer: Anthropology, Advocacy, and Activism*. Rutgers University Press, Rutgers, NJ.

Schlesinger, Stephen C., and Stephen Kinzer. 1990. *Bitter Fruit: The Untold Story of the American Coup in Guatemala*. Doubleday, New York.

Seguridad, Justicia y Paz. 2015. "Por cuarto año consecutivo, San Pedro Sula es la ciudad más violenta del mundo." January 20, 2015. http://www .seguridadjusticiaypaz.org.mx/sala-de-prensa/1165-por-cuarto-ano-consecutivo -san-pedro-sula-es-la-ciudad-mas-violenta-del-mundo.

Sev'er, Aysan. 1999. "Exploring the Continuum: Sexualized Violence by Men and Male Youth against Women and Girls." *Atlantis: Critical Studies in Gender, Culture and Social Justice* 24(1): 95–104.

Sieder, Rachel. 2002. "Recognizing Indigenous Law and the Politics of State Formation in Meso-America." In *Multiculturalism in Latin America: Indigenous Rights, Diversity and Democracy*, ed. Rachel Sieder, 184–207. Palgrave, New York.

Sierra, María Teresa, and Rachel Sieder. 2010. "Indigenous Women's Access to Justice in Latin America." CMI Working Paper WP 2010: 2. Chr. Michelsen Institute, Bergen. https://www.cmi.no/publications/3880-indigenous-womens -access-to-justice-in-latin.

Simanski, John F. 2014. *Annual Report: Immigration Enforcement Actions: 2013*. Department of Homeland Security Office of Immigration Statistics, Washington,

DC. https://www.dhs.gov/sites/default/files/publications/Enforcement_Actions
_2013.pdf.

Simanski, John F., and Lesley M. Sapp. 2012. *Annual Report: Immigration Enforcement
Actions: 2011*. Department of Homeland Security Office of Immigration Statistics,
Washington, DC. https://www.dhs.gov/sites/default/files/publications
/Enforcement_Actions_2011.pdf.

Simpson, Audra. 2014. *Mohawk Interruptus: Political Life across the Borders of Settler
States*. Duke University Press, Durham, NC.

———. 2016. "The State Is a Man: Theresa Spence, Loretta Saunders and the
Gender of Settler Sovereignty." *Theory and Event* 19(4).

Smith, Andrea. 2005. *Conquest: Sexual Violence and American Indian Genocide*. South
End Press, Cambridge, MA.

Smith, Linda Tuhiwai. 1996. *Decolonizing Methodologies: Research and Indigenous
Peoples*. Zed Books, London.

Sokoloff, Natalie J., and Ida Dupont. 2005. "Domestic Violence at the Intersections
of Race, Class, and Gender: Challenges and Contributions to Understanding
Violence against Marginalized Women in Diverse Communities." *Violence against
Women* 11(1): 38–64.

Speed, Shannon. 2005. "Dangerous Discourses: Human Rights and Multiculturalism
in Mexico." *PoLAR: Political and Legal Anthropology Review* 28(1): 29–51.

———. 2006. "At the Crossroads of Human Rights and Anthropology: Toward
a Critically Engaged Activist Research." *American Anthropologist* 108(1):
66–77.

———. 2007. "The Zapatista Juntas de Buen Gobierno: Exercising rights,
Reconfiguring resistance." *The Practice of Human Rights: Tracking Law in
Transnational Contexts*, ed. Mark Goodale and Sally Merry, 163–92. Cambridge
University Press, Cambridge.

———. 2008a. "Forged in Dialogue: Toward a Critically Engaged Activist Research."
In *Engaging Contradictions: Activist Scholarship in Interdisciplinary Perspective*, ed.
Charles R. Hale, 213–36. University of California Press, Berkeley.

———. 2008b. *Rights in Rebellion: Indigenous Struggle and Human Rights in Chiapas*.
Stanford University Press, Stanford, CA.

———. 2014. "A Dreadful Mosaic: Rethinking Gender Violence through the Lives of
Indigenous Women Migrants." In "Anthropological Approaches to Gender-Based
Violence and Human Rights," special issue, *Gendered Perspectives on International
Development*, Working Paper No. 304, 78–94.

———. 2016. "States of Violence: Indigenous Women Migrants in the Era of
Neoliberal Multicriminalism." *Critique of Anthropology* 36(3): 280–301.

Speed, Shannon, and María Teresa Sierra. 2005. "Introduction: Critical Perspectives
on Human Rights and Multiculturalism in Neoliberal Latin America." *PoLAR:
Political and Legal Anthropology Review* 28(1): 1–9.

Stasiulis, Daiva, and Nira Yuval-Davis. 1995. *Unsettling Settler Societies: Articulations of
Gender, Race, Ethnicity and Class*. Sage, London.

Stephen, Lynn. 2007. *Transborder Lives: Indigenous Oaxacans in Mexico, California,
and Oregon*. Duke University Press, Durham, NC.

———. 2013a. "Political Asylum and Gendered Violence among Mexican Immigrant Women in the U.S." Paper prepared for the Annual Congress of the Latin American Studies Association, May 29–June 1, 2013, Washington, DC. Manuscript in the possession of the author.

———. 2013b. *We Are the Face of Oaxaca: Testimony and Social Movements*. Duke University Press, Durham, NC.

———. 2015. "Ser testigo presencial—Acompañando, presenciando, actuando: Martin Diskin Memorial Lecture." *LASA Forum* 46(3): 4–14.

Stoler, Ann. 1995. *Race and the Education of Desire: Foucault's History of Sexuality and the Colonial Order of Things*. Duke University Press, Durham, NC.

Stoll, David. 1999. *Rigoberta Menchu and the Story of All Poor Guatemalans*. Routledge, New York.

Stuesse, Angela. 2016. *Scratching Out a Living: Latinos, Race, and Work in the Deep South*. University of California Press, Berkeley.

Stumpf, Juliet. 2006. "The Crimmigration Crisis: Immigrants, Crime, and Sovereign Power." *American University Law Review* 56:367–419.

Suzack, Cheryl, Shari M. Huhndorf, Jeanne Perreault, and Jean Barman, eds. 2010. *Indigenous Women and Feminism: Politics, Activism, Culture*. UBC Press, Vancouver.

Terrazas, Aaron. 2010. "Mexican Immigrants in the United States." Migration Policy Institute. https://www.migrationpolicy.org/article/mexican-immigrants-united -states-2.

Tomsho, Robert. 1987. *The American Sanctuary Movement*. Texas Monthly Press, Austin.

Tsing, Anna. 2015a. *The Mushroom at the End of the World: On the Possibility of Life in Capitalist Ruins*. Princeton University Press, Princeton, NJ.

———. 2015b. "Salvage Accumulation, or the Structural Effects of Capitalist Generativity." *Cultural Anthropology* website, March 30, 2015. https://culanth.org /fieldsights/656-salvage-accumulation-or-the-structural-effects-of-capitalist -generativity.

United Nations Committee on the Protection of the Rights of All Migrant Workers and Members of Their Families (CMW). 2017. "Concluding Observations on the Third Periodic Report of Mexico." https://tbinternet.ohchr.org/_layouts /treatybodyexternal/Download.aspx?symbolno =CMW%2fC%2fMEX%2fCO%2f3&Lang=en.

United Nations Secretariat of the Permanent Forum on Indigenous Issues. 2007. *Indigenous Women and the UN System: Good Practices and Lessons Learned*. Report for Task Force on Indigenous Women/Interagency Network on Women and Gender Equality. United Nations, New York.

UN Women. 2011. "Guatemala." http://lac.unwomen.org/en/donde-estamos /guatemala.

U.S. Customs and Border Patrol. 2017. "CBP Border Security Report." https://www .cbp.gov/document/annual-report/cbp-border-security-report-fy2017.

U.S. Drug Enforcement Agency. 2016. *2016 National Drug Threat Assessment Summary*. https://www.dea.gov/documents/2016/11/01/2016-national-drug -threat-assessment.

U.S. Government Accountability Office. 2010. *DHS Needs to Comprehensively Assess Its Foreign Language Needs and Capabilities and Identify Shortfalls*. Report to the Subcommittee on Oversight of Government Management, the Federal Workforce, and the District of Columbia, Committee on Homeland Security and Governmental Affairs, U.S. Senate, GAO-10-714. Government Accountability Office, Washington, DC. http://www.gao.gov/assets/310/305850.pdf.

U.S. State Department. 2012. *Trafficking in Persons Report 2012*. U.S. State Department, Washington, DC. http://www.state.gov/j/tip/rls/tiprpt/2012/.

Vacchio, Nick. 2017. "Profiteering from Death: Honduras' War on Indigenous Communities." *Prospect Journal of International Affairs at UCSD*, June 15, 2017. https://prospectjournal.org/2017/06/15/profiteering-from-death-honduras-war-on-indigenous-communities/.

Váldez Cárdenas, Javier. 2011. *Levantones: Historias reales de desaparecidos y víctimas del narco*. Aguilar, Mexico City, Mexico.

Váldez Cárdenas, Javier. 2010. *Miss Narco: Belleza, poder y violencia*. Aguilar, Mexico City.

Van Cott, Donna Lee. 2000. *The Friendly Liquidation of the Past: The Politics of Diversity in Latin America*. University of Pittsburgh Press, Pittsburgh.

———. 2007. "Latin America's Indigenous Peoples." *Journal of Democracy* 18(4): 127–42.

Velasco Ortiz, Laura, and Dolores París Pombo. 2014. "Indigenous Migration in Mexico and Central America: Interethnic Relations and Identity Transformations." *Latin American Perspectives* 41(3): 5–25.

Velasquez Estrada, Ruth Elizabeth. 2017. "Paradoxes of Grassroots Peacemaking: Warrior Masculinity, Violence and Intergenerational Dialogues in Postwar El Salvador," PhD dissertation, University of Texas at Austin (embargoed from publication until 2020).

Velásquez Nimatuj, Irma Alicia. 2013. "Peritaje cultural. Caso: violaciones sexuales a mujeres q'eqchi' en marco del conflict armado interno (1960–1996) de Guatemala caso Sepur Z, muncipio de El Estor, departamento de Izabal. Número de expediente Ministerio Público: MP001-2011-118096." Unpublished manuscript in possession of the author.

———. 2016. "Struggle and Obstacles for Indigenous Women's fight for Justice in Guatemala." Talk presented at the University of Texas at Austin. Unpublished manuscript in possession of the author.

Velásquez Orozco, Laura. 2005. *Mixtec Transnational Identity*. University of Arizona Press, Tucson.

Veracini, Lorenzo. 2013a. "The Other Shift: Settler Colonialism, Israel, and the Occupation." *Journal of Palestine Studies* 42(2): 26–42.

———. 2013b. "What Is the Role of Geography in Sociopolitics?" Southern Perspectives, January 10, 2013. https://www.southernperspectives.net/texts/what-is-the-role-of-geography-in-sociopolitics.

Vimalassery, Manu, Juliana Hu Pegues, and Alyosha Goldstein. 2016. "Introduction: On Colonial Unknowing." *Theory and Event* 19(4).

Vizenor, Gerald. 1999. *Manifest Manners: Narratives on Postindian Survivance*. University of Nebraska Press, Lincoln.

Vogt, Wendy. 2013. "Crossing Mexico: Structural Violence and the Commodification of Undocumented Central American Migrants." *American Ethnologist* 40(4): 764–80.

———. 2015. "The War on Drugs Is a War on Migrants." *Landscapes of Violence* 3(1): article 2.

———. 2016. "Stuck in the Middle with You: The Intimate Labours of Mobility and Smuggling along Mexico's Migrant Route." *Geopolitics* 21(2): 366–86.

Wade, Robert Hunter. 2004. "Is Globalization Reducing Poverty and Inequality?" *World Development* 32(4): 567–89.

Weissman, Deborah M. 2009. "Global Economies and Their Progenies: Theorizing Feminicide in Context." In *Terrorizing Women: Feminicide in the Americas*, ed. Rosa-Linda Fregoso and Cynthia Bejarano, 225–42. Duke University Press, Durham, NC.

White House Office of the Press Secretary. 2014. "Remarks by the President in Address to the Nation on Immigration." November 20, 2014. https:// obamawhitehouse.archives.gov/the-press-office/2014/11/20/remarks-president -address-nation-immigration.

Wilson, Angela Cavender. 1996. "Grandmother to Granddaughter: Generations of Oral History in a Dakota Family." In "Writing about (Writing about) American Indians," special issue, *American Indian Quarterly* 20(1): 7–13.

Wilson, Angela Waziyatawin, and Michael Yellow Bird, eds. 2005. *For Indigenous Eyes Only*. School of American Research, Santa Fe.

———, eds. 2012. *For Indigenous Minds Only: A Decolonization Handbook*. School of American Research, Santa Fe.

Wing, Adrien Katherine. 1996. "A Critical Race Feminist Conceptualization of Violence: South African and Palestinian Women." *Albany Law Review* 60:943–74.

Wolfe, Patrick. 1998. *Settler Colonialism and the Transformation of Anthropology: The Politics and Poetics of an Ethnograph Event*. Continuum Press, New York.

———. 2016. *Traces of History: Elementary Structures of Race*. Verso, London.

Women's Commission for Refugee Women and Children and Lutheran Immigration and Refugee Service. 2007. *Locking Up Family Values: The Detention of Immigrant Families*. Women's Commission for Refugee Women and Children, New York; Lutheran Immigration and Refugee Service, Baltimore. https://www .womensrefugeecommission.org/component/zdocs/document/150-locking-up -family-values-the-detention-of-immigrant-families-locking-up-family-values -the-detention-of-immigrant-families.

Yasher, Deborah. 1999. "Democracy, Indigenous Movements, and Postliberal Challenge in Latin America." *World Politics* 52(1): 76–104.

Yellow Bird, Michael. 2005. "Tribal Critical Thinking Centers." In *For Indigenous Eyes Only*, ed. Angela Waziyatawin Wilson and Michael Yellow Bird, 9–30. School of American Research, Santa Fe.

Zilberg, Elana. 2011. *Space of Detention: The Making of a Transnational Gang Crisis between Los Angeles and San Salvador*. Duke University Press, Durham, NC.

Index

Information in figures and tables is indicated by page numbers in *italics*.

colonialism: administrative, 18; anthropology and, 8, 125n8; eliminations and, 19–20; gendered violence and, 34, 35, 40; and ideological construction of indigenous women, 34; and indirect rule, 21; internal, 22–23; labor and, 19; land dispossession and, 19, 20; with land vs. labor, 19; in Latin America, as nonsettler, 19; legacy of, 125n8; metropole, 18, 21; Native writings and, 9; and North/South distinction, 14–15; racial categories and, 23; racialization and, 15, 23, 36, 125n8; sexual violence and, 35; in United States, 15–16, 128n26. *See also* settler colonialism
coloniality of power, 125n8
colonial necropolitics, 34
Committee on the Protection of the Rights of All Migrant Workers and Members of Their Families (CMW), 61, 64
Community Initiatives for Visiting Immigrants in Confinement, 85
Congressional Progressive Caucus, 78
continuum of violence, 29–30
Convention Relating to the Status of Refugees, 81
corporations, private prison. *See* Corrections Corporation of America (CCA); GEO Group
Corrections Corporation of America (CCA), 68, 70, 72, 75, 132n5
Cortes, Hernando, 20
Costa Rica, 24
coyote, 45, 86, 93, 130n1
Crenshaw, Kimberlé, 18, 30, 31, 90
criollo, 21, 23
Crosby, Alison, 37

DACA. *See* Deferred Action for Childhood Arrivals (DACA)
Das, Veena, 29, 40
Das Gupta, Monisha, 103

deferred action, 106, 108, 109, 136n12
Deferred Action for Childhood Arrivals (DACA), 109
"definitional vertigo," 29
De Genova, Nicolas, 102, 105, 127n17, 135–36n11
De Leon, Jason, 13, 65–66, 97
Deloria, Vine, Jr., 7, 8, 126n10
democratization, 3–4, 47–48
Department of Homeland Security (DHS), 70, 73–74, 85
deportability, 97–103
deportation, 52, 55, 87–88, 93–97, 136n18
detention. *See* incarceration
DHS. *See* Department of Homeland Security (DHS)
disciplinary assimilation, 38, 129n4
domestic violence, 1, 2, 31–34; and "definitional vertigo," 29; gang violence and, 54–55; as ground for asylum, 113; and intersectionality theory, 30, 33; reporting of, 101–102; state violence and, 30, 36; stories of, 31–32, 33–34, 35–36; structural violence and, 30–31; ubiquity of, 28. *See also* gender violence
Drug Lord (Poppa), 59
Dunn, Donald, 74–75

economic reorientation, 3
Eighteenth Street Gang, 51, 55
eliminations, 13, 15, 19–26, 40–44, 71, 110, 116, 117
El Salvador, 5, 24, 52, 56, 125n4
encomienda, 20–21
End of History and the Last Man, The (Fukuyama), 125n2
Enhanced Border Security and Visa Entry Reform Act, 132n2
entrepreneurial citizenship, 26
erasure, 12–13, 88–89
eroticization, 11
eugenics, 37
exceptionalism, American, 6

expited removal, 95–96, 108, 132n6
extractivism, 26, 57, 130n7

family detention: conditions in, 72, 78;
ending of, 74; reinstatement of, 76,
95. *See also* T. Don Hutto immigration
facility
fear assessment, 93, 97, 99–100, 132n6
Feingold, David, 103–104
"Felt Theory" (Million), 10
feminicide, 5, 11, 42–43, 65. *See also*
gender violence
First Nations, 10. *See also* Canada
Flores v. Meese, 74, 81
for-profit prison corporations. *See*
Corrections Corporation of America
(CCA); GEO Group
Fox, Vicente, 63
Fukuyama, Francis, 125n2

gang violence, 2; deportation and, 52;
feminicide and, 42; in Guatemala,
57–58; in Honduras, 55; in Mexico,
48–56, 58–59, 60–61; police and, 53,
60; removal of, as reason for asylum,
113; state violence and, 59–60; in
stories, 35–36, 54; trains and, 52–53;
youth, 51. *See also* cartels
Gee, Dolly M., 81–82
gender violence: anthropology and, 11;
and continuum of violence, 29–30;
and "definitional vertigo," 29; in
detention, 74–75, 77–78, 84–86;
feminist theories of, 29; incidence of,
16; Indigenous women's risk for, 16,
17; and intersectionality theory, 29;
lack of accountability for, 42; in
Mexico, 16–17, 64; power relations
and, 39; state violence and, 64. *See
also* domestic violence; feminicide;
sexual violence
General Allotment Act, 37
genocidal moments, 34–42
genocide: in Guatemala, 24, 38–39
GEO Group, 70, 132n5

Gilman, Denise, 80–81
Gledhill, John, 47
globalization, 47, 116
Goeman, Mishuana, 9
Goldstein, Alyosha, 128n26
Goodman, Sam, 11
Gordon, Todd, 56
Gott, Richard, 22
Grassroots Leadership, 6, 108
Guatemala, 1, 3, 21; assimilation in,
37–38; gang violence in, 57–58;
genocide in, 24, 38–39; land
dispossession in, 37–38; La Violencia
period in, 38–39, 129n5; Mexico vs.,
24; number of apprehensions in,
125n4; racialization in, 37; state
violence in, 36–37; United States
and, 38
Guerreros Unidos, 60
Gutierrez, Natividad, 23
Guzmán, Joaquín "El Chapo," 65,
132n21

Hale, Charles, 4, 38, 129n4
Hard Choices (Clinton), 57
Hernández, Rosalva Aída, 62
Heyman, Josiah, 135n5
Homeland Security Act, 70
Honduras, 24; coup in, 130n3; gang
violence in, 55, 56; murders in, 55;
number of apprehensions in, 125n4;
state violence in, 130n7
Hope, Alejandro, 65
Huhndorf, Shari M., 34
hunger strike, 68, 78, 79, 119
Hutto Visitation Program, 6–7
Hutto Visitation Project, 108

ICE. *See* Immigration and Customs
Enforcement (ICE)
iceboxes, 68, 132n1
illiteracy, 50, 96, 100
Immigration and Customs Enforcement
(ICE), 70–71, 73–74, 79–80, 94,
109–110, 135–36n11

Secure Border Initiative, 70
Secure Communities program, 135n10
Security and Prosperity Partnership of
    North America, 132n2
September 11 attacks, 69–70, 94
Sessions, Jeff, 113–114
settler, as term, 127n19
settler capitalism: carcerality and,
    90; and liminality of Indigenous
    women migrants, 14; and structural
    violence, 18; structural violence and,
    18; vulnerability and, 2–3, 91
settler colonialism: capitalism and, 24;
    deportation and, 103; displacement
    and, 20; elimination and, 35; and
    internal colonialism, 23; in Latin
    America, 22; precepts of, 18; as term,
    127n19; vulnerability and, 2
settler state, 112–119
settler tropes, 34–42
sexual violence: in detention centers,
    74–75, 77–78, 85; in Guatemala's La
    Violencia, 38–39, 129n5; and settler
    colonialism, 35; and state power, 34.
    See also gender violence
Simpson, Audra, 34–35
Sinaloa cartel, 60
slavery, 20–21, 90, 104
Smith, Andrea, 34
social Darwinism, 37
social welfare programs, 3
Sonoran Desert, 107
South Africa, 30
Space of Detention (Zilberg), 51–52
"State Is a Man, The" (Simpson),
    34–35
state violence: domestic violence and,
    30, 36; gang violence and, 59–60;
    gender violence and, 64; in
    Guatemala, 36–37; in Honduras,
    130n7; and Mexico, 62–66; in Mexico,
    40–41
Stephen, Lynn, 10
Stoll, David, 126n10
structural violence, 17–18, 30–31

Student and Exchange Visitor
    Information System, 132n2
Suazo, Luis Javier Prince, 130n4
surveillance, 127n17
survivance, 119
Suzack, Cheryl, 34
Syria, 65

Tang, Eric, 6
T. Don Hutto immigration facility, 1,
    6–7, 72–76, 73, 75, 108
Texans United for Families, 6, 73–74,
    108
trafficking, 103–106
trains, 52–53
Transit of Empire, The (Byrd), 18
Trump, Donald, 106, 109, 112, 113–114,
    115–116, 136n18
trust relationships, 26

underemployment, 30–31, 57
unemployment, 30–31, 57
United Nations Declaration on the
    Rights of Indigenous Peoples, 26
United States: colonialism in, 15–16,
    128n26; contestation over indigeneity
    in, 88, 127n18, 135n38; and democ-
    ratization, 3; elimination in, 23;
    exceptionalism, 6; gang violence and,
    52; Guatemala and, 38; as homeland
    security state, 69–72; Honduras and,
    56; and neoliberal multiculturalism,
    6; opioid addiction in, 65; resurgence
    of white supremacy in, 27; trafficking
    within, 104–105; tribes in, 12, 15,
    127n18, 135n38; trust relationships
    in, 26
U.S. Visitor and Immigrant Status
    Indicator Technology program, 132n2

Vasconcelos, José, 129n6
Vásquez Velásquez, Romeo, 130n4
Velasquez, Elizabeth, 52
Velasquez Nimatuj, Irma Alicia, 38–39,
    129n5

Veracini, Lorenzo, 20, 35, 128n1
Victims of Trafficking and Violence
    Protection Act, 104
violence: continuum of, 29–30; legal, 14;
    socially organized, 47–61; structural,
    17–18, 30–31. *See also* domestic
    violence; gang violence; gender
    violence; sexual violence; state
    violence
Violence and the Limits of Representation
    (Matthews and Goodman), 11
visitation programs, 6, 108
Vizenor, Gerald, 119
Vogt, Wendy, 13, 46, 51, 98
vulnerability, 2–3, 12, 41, 91–93, 98,
    114, 126n14

vulnerability-agency dichotomy, 3
vulneradas, 3

"war on drugs," 62, 63, 65
"war on terror," 4
Webber, Jeffery R., 56
"whitening decrees," 37
Wilkinson, Tracy, 57
writing, about trauma, 11–12

Zapatista uprising, 22, 40
Zapotecos, 13
Zayas, Luis, 83–84
Zelaya, Manuel, 56, 57
Zetas cartel, 60
Zilberg, Elana, 51–52

CPSIA information can be obtained
at www.ICGtesting.com
Printed in the USA
LVHW110719151222
735278LV00005B/293